Annie's Child

Annie's Child

✦

Memories of Racism
on the Journey to Hawaii

Hollis Earl Johnson

iUniverse, Inc.
New York   Bloomington

Annie's Child
Memories of Racism on the Journey to Hawaii

iUniverse books may be ordered through booksellers or by contacting:

iUniverse
1663 Liberty Drive
Bloomington, IN 47403
www.iuniverse.com
1-800-Authors (1-800-288-4677)

ISBN: 978-1-4401-9632-4 (sc)
ISBN: 978-1-4401-9633-1 (ebook)
ISBN: 978-1-4401-9634-8 (hc)

Printed in the United States of America

iUniverse rev. date: 12/18/2009

Contents

1

Preface

Recently, there was a congressional push to have reparations made to African Americans for the advent of slavery in America. Many people decried this notion, including myself, but the idea has some merit, since in the past the federal government has paid reparations to Japanese Americans and their descendants for forcing them into prison camps.

In July 2008, the U.S. House of Representatives approved a resolution issuing an apology to African Americans for the fundamental injustice, cruelty, brutality, and inhumanity of slavery and Jim Crow segregation. In February 2008, the U.S. Senate apologized for atrocities committed against American Indians, and previously, in 2005, the Senate apologized for standing by during a lynching campaign against African Americans throughout much of the past century.

Near the end of the twentieth century, Congress apologized for interning Japanese Americans in concentration camps during World War II and issued reparations to the internees and their descendants. Congress had years before considered a similar apology for those victims of the slavery and Jim Crow eras of America, a gesture long sought by African Americans. Such efforts were always bogged down by concerns that the apology would prompt a call for greater reparations.

In recent years, African American activists seeking reparations for slavery have gotten private companies, including banks, insurers, and railroads, to apologize for their role in bankrolling, insuring, capturing, and transporting slaves. In 2005, television news broadcasts and national newspapers reported that one bank Wachovia Corporation had acquired had put thousands of slaves to work on a railroad. That same year, JPMorgan Chase apologized for the role that a subsidiary had played in using ten thousand slaves as collateral and accepting more than one thousand slaves as payments when owners defaulted on loans. Several states, including Virginia, North Carolina, Florida, and Alabama, have issued apologies for slavery.

The "get over it" attitude many Americans display about the subject of slavery only serves to highlight the ignorance of the hurt and the emotional scarring that thousands, perhaps millions, of people from past generations still carry inside. Although my generation did not endure slavery itself, the emotional pain was communicated through generations of African Americans whose relatives survived the atrocious slave ship rides to the North and South American continents.

Annie's Child

Acknowledgments

Dedicated to the memory of one of my best friends in life and my mentor in literature, the late John Black, of Honolulu, Hawaii, who, by our communication, gave me the incentive to write this autobiography. John Black also played a primary role in helping me write an article on the presence of racism in the U.S. military during the 1960s, which was published in the Honolulu *Star-Bulletin* for Memorial Day 2003.

I have included written material from other publishers, such as newspaper writings and excerpts from certain books and magazines, in this autobiography. All information from these sources will be in "fair use" within the narrative. These writings have been included because they record some racially divisive subject or event that has had a profound effect on me.

To Linda, a Latino, who gave me insight into racism she has suffered during her lifetime as an American citizen.

To my co-worker Nina, who tutored me in the local culture.

To Nancy, who will always be my dear friend.

To Katherine, the Great, who shared with me how much emotional pain she suffered as a person of Filipino and African American mixed race.

To my beloved children, Andrea and Jay, this autobiography should help to explain some of the choices I have made in my lifetime and to show the often unrecognized, emotional scarring of racism.

To my grandchildren, Ashleigh, Adam, and Justin, I sincerely regret that I have never had the chance, for various reasons, to meet you. I missed the opportunity of a close grandparent relationship with you. But I celebrate the fact that you would not exist if not for the love of two people, your grandmother Patricia and your grandfather Hollis. You are each a reward for that love.

To my life partner, Tina Ting Hu, thank you for your assistance with this writing.

To my generation, who witnessed the American racial revolution, suffered their own pain, and still carry the emotional scars that will never heal with the "get over it" attitude communicated by many in American society.

To the Little Rock Nine— children of the American civil rights movement of 1950s America. The courage you displayed had a terrific impact on me. I am one of millions of African American people watching who felt your pain.

And to Annie Clara McNair Johnson, who gave me the inner strength to overcome racism. I am Annie's child.

III

Introduction

To My Reader:

This autobiography is written to the present, past, and future generations of American people to reveal the effects of racial injustice. If the reality of racial differences is made known, perhaps we will come to the point where we can start rectifying the absurdity of racism in American society.

Mother Annie is not the only subject of this autobiography. I simply wish to pay tribute to her and to her strength and guidance in my young life. Her guidance was a shield in my struggle to endure the emotional scarring of racism. Mother Annie's emotional strength came from her parents. My grandmother and grandfather, who were of different races, risked their lives by marrying in Mississippi in the years when the Ku Klux Klan would hang people for miscegenation. Mother Annie attempted to pass that strength on to her eight children. And now, having a lifetime of experience with people from many countries and cultures, I can take a macro view of racism in any form.

Although there may be historical and chronological inaccuracies in this autobiography, the narrative is meant to explain the emotional pain inherited from a hostile period in an American revolution.

Part One
Revelation

1

Hollis Earl Johnson

I grew up in Chester, Pennsylvania. In the 1950s, I was considered different because of my race, my biological heritage, and because of social and legal injustice. Even as a young child, I was aware that I was biracial—multiracial, in fact, American Choctaw Indian, African American, and Irish. My grandfather was Irish. My grandmother was both African American and Choctaw Indian. My grandfather and grandmother managed to defy the miscegenation laws of Mississippi, marry, and raise twelve children.

My father and mother, one of the twelve children, met in the mountains near Jackson, Mississippi, where the family was residing. My mother and father married, and I was born in Meridian, Mississippi, shortly before America was thrust into World War II. My parents migrated to Chester, Pennsylvania, during the war years to find a better life. They chose Chester, Pennsylvania, because of the opportunity for my father to make substantially more money working in the shipyards to support the war effort. We lived in Flower Hill, Chester Township, Chester, Pennsylvania. I grew up there, a place that would later become known locally as a ghetto. The nickname "Flower Hill" came from the fact that the neighborhood was located at the top of Engle and Flower streets.

2

Awareness

I grew up with a lot of love that Mother Annie bestowed on all eight of her children. When I was a teenager, I remember my mother telling me of being on a train with her when I was three. We were heading to Pennsylvania to be with my father. She told me that we had been sitting in the "colored only" section of that train. The African American soldiers on that train had been teasing my mother because she had a black child and looked white, and because she was a beautiful woman—the last beautiful American woman they might see before going to war. My mother told me the soldiers had wondered what a white woman was doing sitting in the "colored only" section of the train. I remember her tears in the dark as she told me about our train ride and her hugging me so tightly so she couldn't be heard crying. I remember her saying, "I love you," so softly. I remember.

Growing up in Chester Township was not easy. Looking back now, it was isolated, but my mother, Annie Clara McNair Johnson, and my father, Tommie Lee Johnson, tried their best not to let me see life in the township as separate from the rest of Chester. My father and mother toiled day and night, working to support their children. The kids kept coming, from their love, as I understand now. Papa worked in the shipyards to support the brood. Mom did domestic work. In the meantime, they kept teaching all of us about life and its obstacles. My mother and father provided a home full of love for their family.

Like most children, I could not imagine a world beyond the pretty eyes of Mama. I will never forget my first day of school. Mother Annie hugged me so tightly before we walked out the door. Looking back, I can see that she was saying good-bye to her baby.

That morning, as we walked to the school, I did not realize my mother was sending me on my life journey. All the way to the school, I could feel her love in her tight touch. As we approached the school entrance, she stooped down, held me, and said, "This is the best I could ever give you." She kissed me and told me to go in. I could not understand why she had pushed me away. I felt so hurt at that moment. When she walked away, I felt so lonely, like I was losing a part of myself. Now I understand that a mother's love has no equal.

My life took off from there. There were a lot of trying times.

On one particular occasion, I had to learn about responsibility the hard way. I was responsible for feeding my baby sister in her high chair, and I remember feeling utterly devastated when I almost killed her because of my negligence. She swallowed one of those little can openers manufacturers used to add to their packaging while I was trying to feed her in the high chair. I did not notice that somehow the opener had gotten into her food because I was too busy looking at that new phenomenon—the television. Anita, my baby sister, survived after a hospital stay, but I felt so much guilt because she was my responsibility. I feel that same guilt even to this day when I think of her or see her because I failed to keep her safe. Over the years, I have learned about the frailty of life—especially after seeing the carnage and death as part of the U.S. military mission in Vietnam, and the fact that I put my little sister in danger has left an indelible mark.

There were a total of eight kids: me, Hollis Earl; Tommie Jean; Brook Fontaine; Leslie Andrew; Timothy Leon; Teresa Ann; Anita Louise; and Doreen Michele. The sister born after me, Jean, was my dearest friend. We were so close, mainly because we endured a lot together in taking care of our siblings, the housecleaning, the cooking, and completing homework together.

One night, Jean had a toothache so bad I convinced her to go with me to a local dentist, who had an office in his home, which was within walking distance. We left in the middle of the night to go see him, not informing Mom and Dad. Her pain was so intense that I had to wipe away her tears on the way to the dentist's house. The dentist treated her, but when we returned home, we were confronted by Mom and Dad about where we had been. Apparently, they had heard us leave the house. I explained the situation, and as Papa ranted on about us not informing them, tears formed in Mama's eyes as she gave Jean a big hug. The pain from Jean's tooth left later that week, and Jean was back to her normal, energetic self. We began telling each other our secrets and sharing our emotions, which taught us more about ourselves and the people around us.

Growing up in Chester Township was isolated from the reality of racial differences. My earliest recognition of racial differences came from the black-and-white television screen. The only black people on television in those days were white men mimicking African Americans with black face paint and typecast voices. These were the characters for the *Amos 'n' Andy* show, which later introduced African Americans playing the parts. The *Nat King Cole Show* was to come later. The *Nat King Cole Show* ended after a short run because of existing racial prejudices. No large company would sponsor a black star on national television. I also began to recognize racial differences with my mother, her sister Beatrice, and a German lady who was a neighbor. My aunt Beatrice had also migrated to Chester Township from Mississippi. Gossip was that our German neighbor and her African American husband met and married in Germany after World War II, during the American occupation. He was a dark-skinned man, and I could identify them with my mother and father as black and white. There were other white faces daily. There was a grocery store— which I learned later was a typical business in African American communities during those years—that was owned and operated by Jewish people. One of the most stunning revelations about racial differences came to me as a teenager in the early 1950s, when I first laid eyes on my aunt Dora, who is only a few years older than me. I was taking my usual stroll from Perry A. Wright Elementary School to my home, not far away. As I approached the walkway to the front door of our house, the most beautiful white woman I had ever seen—other than Mom, of course—came walking down the walkway and said, "Hello, Hollis." I was stunned by her beauty and familiarity. My aunt Dora had also migrated to Chester, Pennsylvania, from Mississippi. It was also about the time when I actually began to understand the teasing from most of the other kids in the community. The teasing about my white mother and white relatives began to hurt my feelings a little.

America was in the early stages of a racial revolution when I was a young teen. I was born in 1941, and as a teenager I became aware of the struggle for racial equality for African American people in the United States. My mother and father were adamant in teaching us kids that no people are better than any others because of racial, cultural, or ethnic differences. However, the disparity of treatment that was given to African Americans through the unfair laws and attitudes that were pervasive in American society at the time was obvious. My mother was working as a domestic housekeeper for a well-known wealthy family, and she had to separate me from being too close to their daughter, Kathleen, who was the same age as me, because the two of us were of different races. We were good friends and loved talking to each other when I went to her house with my mother. Those were the summer months, and Mom took the opportunity of taking me away from the township isolation on occasion. Kathleen and I enjoyed our time together, and we were always under the supervision of my mother. One day, while we were sitting on the outside steps talking, I noticed lawn gnomes in many of the neighborhood yards that were designed to look like little black men with lanterns. "Why do people have those lawn gnomes in their yards?" I asked.

Kathleen frowned. "My parents told me that the statues were a way for the neighbors to tell that black people worked here. It keeps the neighbors from calling the police if they see colored people around a house."

Many questions raced through my mind after she told me about the statues. Later I learned the view that many white people had of "Negroes," as we were called in those years. I gained a lot of insight about how many white people felt about people of color in the short time that she and I were allowed to converse with each other. She also learned things from me that dispelled some of the myths she had gathered about the status of black people in America. Her basic understanding at that age was that black people were inferior to white people. We spent a couple summers talking about different things. Mother Annie made sure we didn't get too deep into the racial discussions, though. How much could we know at that age? Then later, when it was time to go back to school, Mother Annie told me that she could no longer take me to her employers' house because Kathleen's parents thought we were getting too friendly for our racial difference. I never saw her again after that summer. I was twelve or thirteen when it happened, and what my mother told me was really painful. But years later I realized that her parents were judging us kids through their own prejudices and the status quo of American societal values.

Back in the township, one of the strangest things at that time was noticing that one of the older African American guys living in the neighborhood was hanging out with white friends across Engle Street. Engle Street was the unspoken segregation line for white and black Chester Township. This particular fellow—James—could be seen in restaurants and other establishments that catered to white people. He was very popular with his white friends. I never saw James associating with any African Americans. His friends would drop him off at the Engle Street border in their cars. They would never venture into his side of the township. He was accepted as one of the gang—up to a point. His behavior confused me. James valued white friendship more than having African American friends.

In January, America observes Martin Luther King Jr. Day. Each year, in the mention of his birthday, I remember another event that made me aware of racial divisions. Mom and Pop took me to a church meeting. It was a sermon by the Reverend Dr. Martin Luther King Jr. At the time, Dr. King was a ministerial student. I will never forget the passion of that sermon. After that sermon, I became aware of a big problem in America. Before that time, I had not been aware of the strong racial segregation in the South. Dr. King's sermon explained the pain of living with segregation and the separation of the races by the government— unfair laws that were applied unequally by race and that affected education, health care, employment, transportation, housing, and crime and punishment, to name a few.

I remember shaking Dr. King's hand at the door as we were leaving the church. Years later, I would see him again.

In 1955, I became aware of the news on television concerning a city transit bus boycott by African Americans in Alabama. A lone African American woman in Montgomery, Alabama, defied a law that African Americans must sit farther back in the bus in deference to white passengers. What did this mean? Living in my little township, television was all I could rely on for a view into the world. I discovered that African Americans were boycotting the bus company because of an unjust law. The broadcast went on to report that it was the African Americans who were spending the most money and who were the best revenue for the bus company owners! This event stirred up many questions inside of me. I remember asking, "How can they do that? It's so wrong!" My mother and father sat with me one evening and tried to answer my questions. That conversation made me realize that racism was embedded deep within American society, in addition to the open, racist dogma in some areas of the country.

My mother and father ended the conversation by conveying their passion—that people are not to be judged by their differences but the content of their character. I believe it was my parents' way of ensuring that I did not harbor hatred in my heart.

A little later on in my teen years in Chester Township, I became conscious of other things that began to shape my racial awareness. A friend of my mother and father, a sworn township policeman, explained to me that the reason I saw only African American policemen in the township was because that was the local understanding to prevent problems. "What problems?" I wondered. The law is the law. But as I tried to sleep that night, the problem in Alabama surfaced in my brain. Why were white people judging African Americans so differently? Was it because we looked different than them?

Later in my youth, I heard of a horrible murder in Mississippi, where I was born. A young African American boy about my age, Emmett Till, was brutally murdered by someone—allegedly a local white store owner—because Till said something disrespectful to the store owner's wife, who was working in the store. When I saw the pictures of the brutally murdered boy in an issue of *Jet* magazine, I was stunned, and my emotions were beginning to become very affected by others' racist hatred. I had no idea of how African Americans had suffered in the past in America; I was not aware of the history. There was no African American history taught in American schools in those days; and not much at all in American high schools.

3

Heritage

My father's parents were slaves from Nigeria. My maternal grandmother was both Choctaw American Indian and African American. The Choctaw Indian Nation were Floridians who were assigned to reservations in different states, including Mississippi. My grandmother's African American heritage came from her father, a "Buffalo" soldier serving with a unit in that area. The African American soldiers were nicknamed by American Indians as "Buffalo" soldiers during the early Indian wars. My understanding is the name was given by the Indians because the black soldiers had hair similar to that of the buffalo, a treasured animal to the Indian nations.

My grandmother, who was both Native and African American, lived on the reservation and met my grandfather because of a railroad line that passed through the Choctaw Indian reservation. My grandfather was a descendant of Irish parents. I was told by Mother Annie that my grandfather was a conductor on the train. My grandmother and grandfather loved each other so much that they decided to defy the laws of their time against mixed-race marriages. My grandfather, through his earlier experience and travel with the Illinois Central Railroad, had acquired some land in Mississippi that was not easily accessible—on a mountaintop, in fact, or molehill, as they are called in Mississippi—where he and my grandmother lived and bore twelve children. They lived with the reality of racial oppression and the Ku Klux Klan.

I never gained much knowledge of my father's parents. I do remember his sister, who cared for me in Mississippi when I was a small child. Mother Annie never knew much about my father's family, except for his sister, my aunt Lu, and his two brothers who resided in St. Louis. My father's parents had died by the time my mother and father met when they were teenagers. He had joined President Franklin Roosevelt's Civilian Conservation Corps, an organization designed to bring employment to young Americans and to help relieve American families during the Great Depression. My father was employed by that segment of the corps that cut down forests for government building materials. My father was assigned to the mountainous area near where my mother lived, and he used to see her at the edge of my grandfather's property line. They met, continued to see each other, and fell in love. It was from this union, I was conceived.

My heritage became, at times, very hard to face. When my grandfather, my mother's father, came to visit his three daughters living in Chester Township in the early 1950s, I felt very embarrassed about the kids my age teasing me about the "white man" walking the stretch of neighborhood from my mother's sister Bea's house to our house. Even though the kids had seen my aunties and my mother, they still teased me about that "white" man. I did not understand. To me he was a man. I related his skin color to my mother and aunties. The neighborhood kids asked me, "What did your family do wrong to bring a white man to your door?" In those days, to most African Americans living in the township, a white person venturing into the township meant the family they went to see was in trouble of some sort. To most African American kids, the white face was a symbol of punishing authority.

4

The Word Nigger

One time, when I was about eight years old, I was playing with two of the neighborhood kids when we found a book of matches on the ground near a nearby house. We began striking the matches and throwing them around. We accidentally threw one of the matches into a large dumpster near the house and started a fire. When the firemen arrived, they seemed very angry. I noticed that they were all white men. I heard one of the firemen speaking angrily to a person in the house after putting out the fire. As the men were rolling up the fire hoses, one of them said, "I don't know why we have to come over here to help these niggers." It was the first time I gave any recognition to the word *nigger*. What was it? What did that word mean?

As a young teen attending Perry A. Wright School, I started asking questions about the world outside of Chester Township. Racial and cultural differences started to stand out. One day, at school, I asked the teacher a question I should have asked Mother Annie: "What is a nigger?" The whole classroom went silent, and I thought I might have said a curse word. The teacher looked astounded and said she would explain the meaning of the word to me after the class had ended. After class the teacher explained that during slavery the word *nigger* had its origin from the Spanish-speaking slave traders taking captured slaves on board the ships. The Negroid race name "Negro" was altered in translation by the sailors to "nigger." The American slave owners adopted that description to designate slaves. The American slave owners later started using the word in derision of the slaves. Later, I felt so ashamed because my schoolmates teased me because I did not already have this knowledge.

5

Employment Bias

During summer break in 1954 (school breaks at that time were a full three months), I got my first job. I worked as a bowling alley pinsetter. In those days, automatic machine pinsetters were not common, and the only bowling establishment—located in downtown Chester—hired young people to do the job because they could pay them less wages. What I didn't know until I started the job was that the young people were all Caucasian people. I was twelve years old, soon to be thirteen, when a man who lived in our community, William, a janitor at the bowling establishment, told a friend's parents about employment openings for pinsetters. At that time, I was working as an assistant to a friend of mine, Ralph, who was giving me part of the money he earned on his newspaper route. A delivery truck would bring the newspapers to his house each morning. We would deliver them to subscribing households after school each day. On Saturday and Sundays, we would deliver the Chester Times in the early morning.

Ralph and I jumped at the chance to learn to be pinsetters. What Ralph and I didn't know at the time was that we were being considered for hire due to pressure on the local Chester City Council by the county National Association for the Advancement of Colored People (NAACP) and the Urban League to hire "Negroes," as we were called back then, in every segment of Chester's business structure.

My buddy Ralph and I were hired in June that summer. I will never forget the stares of people in the bowling alley while we were being interviewed in an open area of the establishment where patrons and employees could see us. An African American representative for the NAACP and another from the Urban League were there, sitting with my friend and me during the interview. I told my parents that evening that I felt like a celebrity during the interview. Soon we got the news that we were "experiments." My parents assured me that it was for the greater good. Our first night at work was a Monday, and our parents escorted us to work the four to eleven shift. Our parents and the representatives from the Urban League and NAACP stayed at the bowling alley for the entire shift. We had to be trained by the establishment manager because—as we learned later—the other employees refused to train us. We trained on an unused lane at the far end of the alley. The bowlers were our parents and the representatives—everyone else in the alley was white. The manager had put up a curtain separating our lane from the others, so we could not be seen. I learned quickly how to manipulate and reset bowling pins, and within two hours we were fully capable pinsetters, according to the manager.

We soon found out that the ability to jump from one bowling pit to the one next to yours—covering two lanes at once—allowed for restroom trips. We were assigned personal lockers later that night. Ralph and I had lockers next to each other, of course. The next night was an eye-opening experience for me. Ralph and I took a bus to downtown Chester to arrive for the four to eleven shift. The first thing I noticed as we came in was a policeman sitting near the entrance. We found out later he was assigned there for the evening for our protection. As we signed in, the manager told us we were to sit at a table out of sight until there were patrons for all of the alleys. We were instructed not to go to our lockers until that time. Ralph and I complied with the manager's instructions. As other pinsetters and employees came in and signed in for their shift, I noticed most of them came over to stare at us. Some were curious stares, others were sneering and threatening. One guy, another pinsetter, came over to our table and asked belligerently, "Why do you niggers want to work here?" The policeman shouted at him to leave us alone, and the pinsetter walked away. There was that word *nigger* again.

A couple of hours passed, and we were still sitting at that table. The place was filling with customers. Ralph decided he was going to use the restroom. As he stood to walk to the restroom, which was located in the rear of the building, past the bowling lanes, the policeman stopped him and asked where he was going. When Ralph explained that he was going to the restroom, the policeman told him to wait—that he would get an escort for us, which I understood to mean I had to go also. Our escort turned out to be William, the janitor who first made us aware of the bowling jobs. As we walked past the bowling lanes, I could see customers waiting in the backseats; they were there for open and not league bowling. I also noticed the curtain was still up that separated the last two lanes from view. I turned to William. "Why aren't we using the last two lanes for waiting customers?"

He scratched his chin. "The two curtained lanes are for Negro customers only. They hired you to be their pinsetters."

When we arrived at the restroom door, William told us to wait outside while he went in to check. He came back out and said, "Someone's in the restroom. You can't go in until they finish." When I asked why, he said, "Son, this is like the South, so just wait." I had no idea what he meant by that statement. When we went inside, William stood by the door so no one would walk in.

Ralph and I never got a chance to set pins that night. We sat at our table, ate our lunch, watched, and talked for the whole shift. When we were signing out that night, after all the other employees had logged out, the policeman told us he was giving us a ride to the bus stop. When he let us out at the bus stop, he did not leave until we got on the bus. I realized later his assignment that night was to prevent any violence relative to the town's "experiment."

Thinking back on our whole experience that evening, I began to feel an anger building inside me. The next morning, when I told Mother Annie what had happened, I told her I was not going back there. She explained that Ralph and I had been selected for the experiment because of our personalities. And once again she used the words "for the greater good." After she spoke to me about her experiences growing up in Mississippi, I began to truly understand the far-reaching grasp of racism. Mother Annie painted an ugly picture in my mind that morning. She explained that the racial inequalities that existed in America must be changed, and this local experiment was our contribution to that change. I was hurt and confused. However, the determination I felt in my mother's words convinced me to go back. I wanted to strike a blow at the racism my mother had felt in her lifetime. On the bus trip downtown the next day, I learned that Ralph had also told his mom that he did not want to go back to the bowling alley. He too had been told about racial injustice and the importance of this experiment. We were both convinced our scary venture was important.

When we arrived at the bowling alley for our shift, the policeman was again near the entrance. He introduced Ralph and me to the owner, who was standing by him. The night manager was also there. Looking very serious, he asked Ralph and me to meet with the owner in a private office. The policeman came in also. Ralph and I answered several questions from the owner about how we liked our job and if we would stay on for the whole summer. We both said yes. His next question surprised us. He wanted to know if we knew of anyone else who would like to work as pinsetters. He stated that all of the other pinsetters had quit because we were working there. He stated that he did not mind having "colored" pinsetters. Ralph and I promised we would try to recruit other guys from the neighborhood. The owner also stated that he would abide by the law no matter what happened. I wondered what he meant by that statement, but I did not ask him. I found out later.

After our meeting with the owner was finished, Ralph and I were allowed to walk freely around the establishment. I noticed right away that the curtain hiding the last two lanes was gone. A few other white employees came in later—the bowling shoes person, the refreshment counter person, the cashiers and scorekeepers, but no pinsetters. The janitor, William, was also there. William did not escort us to the restroom that night. As the night moved on, no pinsetters checked in for work, and there were very few customers. Ralph and I set pins for open bowling customers for about four hours that night. Some of the bowlers left very large tips for us. I was surprised, because the customers were all white. William informed Ralph and I that all the pinsetters had called in to say they were quitting if Ralph and I got hired. The owner had instructed his managers to tell them that he had no choice because of law. I felt a sense of rejection, shame, and victory that night.

As the night moved on and after about two hours with no customers, the owner decided to close the place for the night. I heard him tell the policeman, "I'm going to lose a lot of money because of these guys." The policeman just laughed and suggested he sell the place to "colored" people. The policeman took us to the bus stop and wished us luck, because he would not be at the bowling establishment again, unless they got a call. On the bus that night, Ralph and I were silent. By the end of the following week, all the pinsetters at the bowling alley were African American. But the most amazing thing for me was that by the end of the summer, we had both black and white customers at the bowling alley.

But what remained from that experience was the pain that I felt from being rejected because of my race. My self-awareness and self-esteem was crippled that summer.

6

African American Status

Another venture into racial acceptance in America came during because of the law. On our walk home from school one day, a friend asked me to join him in distributing two magazines, *Ebony* and *Jet*, to subscribers. I had never heard of these magazines before. But I learned later, after accepting my friend's invitation, that these magazines were sold nationally and gave the African Americans in the township insight into African American concerns and events in America. I also discovered a newspaper called the *Pittsburg Courier*, which related African American concerns and events nationally. The first day I started distributing the *Ebony* and *Jet* magazines, I noticed the welcoming look local people gave us when we made the deliveries. That night, I took the extra copies home to show my parents. They told me they were aware of the magazines but could not afford a subscription. As I read the magazines that night, I began to understand the need African Americans had for the magazines. I also thought it was oxymoronic that we were subscribing to the *Chester Times* daily newspaper, which was a cheaper insight into a world outside of Chester Township. As I continued reading *Ebony* and *Jet*, I became aware of events that made African American people speak so poorly of white people, including the murders (lynching) of African Americans by white people; sharecropper abuses by white people; employment discrimination; and back of the bus laws in southern states. But because of my parents, my emotions remained neutral. I remember Mother Annie speaking so profoundly on the subject of racial differences. She made a statement I will never forget: "It will never really matter about cultural or physical racial differences if it doesn't matter to you."

By reading *Ebony* and *Jet*, I became more aware of the structure and goals of organizations like the NAACP and the National Urban League. I also learned the details of historical events concerning African Americans from reading these magazines. In 1954, I became aware that a historic U.S. Supreme Court decision had been made, affecting the de facto segregation trend in the American school system. This was the *Brown v. Topeka, Kansas* case. The case involved an African American little girl who was forced to attend a segregated elementary school, located miles from where she lived, when there was an elementary school located just a few blocks from her home. The Supreme Court ruled against racial segregation of schools and school districts and explained that it violated the Constitution of the United States.

What did this mean? I began to learn about the groundbreaking significance of this Supreme Court decision from listening to adults and reading the newspapers and magazines. In my existence in Chester Township, I had been unaware of what was happening in the outside world. That was about to change!

The bus boycott in Montgomery, Alabama, was the beginning of my understanding the issues of state and national laws. I learned that one person—just like the little girl in the case of *Brown v. Topeka, Kansas* and like Mrs. Rosa Parks, who was honored decades later by the president for sparking change in American society—can make a difference. By Mrs. Parks refusing to give up her seat on a Montgomery, Alabama, city bus to a white person, a revolution was given a historical precedence.

I also experienced the pain of segregation when I went on a holiday trip to Jackson, Mississippi, during that eighth-grade school year I was walking down a Jackson street with my aunt Dora when a white policeman stopped us. He asked, "Gal, what are doing walking down the street with that nigger boy?"

My aunt Dora then pushed me and said, "Go walk on the other side of the street."

I obeyed, although I was thoroughly perplexed and hurt because I was told by my aunt to follow a distance behind her until we got home. When we got back to Chester Township, I questioned my mother. Mother Annie explained to me that because Aunt Dora looked white, I was not allowed to be seen walking with a white person. The way in which my mother explained that circumstance seemed to be a normal thing to her. It took me a long time to understand and accept the reality, but I have never forgotten the pain.

7

Awakening

After working weekends as a bowling pinsetter in my early teen years, I decided to try to find another job. I started working the next summer at a small clothing store in the bustling shopping area of downtown Chester. Judy, a middle-aged white lady, offered me the job. I had been referred by her housemaid, who knew my family. Judy and I worked together in the store every day that summer except Sundays. I was a stocker and janitor for the store. Sometimes she drove me to her home in the suburbs to do landscaping work for her. Usually Judy's son would drive me back to downtown Chester so I could catch the bus to Flower Hill. She was a very nice lady and was always kind to me. We talked a lot during slow sale periods, and for the second time in my life I was having regular conversations with someone white. When we discussed racial issues, Judy was candid. She believed in racial equality. I sensed her sincerity, and we even ate lunch together most days, which she would bring for both of us from her home. Her husband would come to the store occasionally to do audits. He worked in downtown Philadelphia as an accountant for a law firm. He also made me feel like family when I was around him. Judy's two children, who were attending nearby Swarthmore College, were also very kind.

One particular day, I experienced Judy's sincerity about racism firsthand. That day, for some reason, she was not able to bring in our lunch as usual. She closed the store during the lunch hour and invited me to eat lunch with her at a nearby Woolworth's 5 & 10 cent store.

As we walked down the block, I could see people, black and white, staring at us, and I remembered that day in Mississippi when I was walking down the street with Aunt Dora. The staring continued inside the store. Judy was obviously well-known in downtown Chester. People greeted her, while staring at me. At the lunch counter, people would come up to find out who was sitting next to her. Judy told me not to let their inquisitiveness bother me; that it was something they didn't often see. Some of them recognized me from the store, but they also seemed surprised that I was with her.

Later that day, I overheard a conversation Judy was having with the store owner next door. He must have thought I couldn't hear the conversation because I had been working in the basement storeroom. As I reached the top of the steps, I heard him tell her, "Where I come from, white women don't walk around having lunch with colored boys."

As I started back down the basement steps, because I didn't want them to know I had overheard, I heard her say angrily, "We are not where you come from."

I stayed in the basement for at least another half hour arranging boxes before I came back up the stairs. Judy was waiting on customers when I went by to work in the rear storage room. Later that day, near closing time, I noticed that she looked flustered, red in the face and very quiet. I knew she was upset, so I admitted that I had heard the conversation and apologized. I told her, "I don't have to come back, if you want."

Judy opened her mouth in shock and brushed away my suggestion. "No, don't say that! You remember, you should never bow to people like that." Then she said, "My husband will have a talk with him." She asked if she could give me a ride home instead of me taking the bus.

I was surprised and said yes. I knew she was concerned for my safety. I was more concerned for her taking me home, because where I lived was not beautiful in comparison to where she lived. As Judy drove me home, she revealed that she had grown up near the township in Chichester, Pennsylvania. And she knew the township area very well.

She could remember that during WWII the shipyards were short of employees due to the surge in demand for ships to support the war effort. She remembered that shipyards started recruiting Negroes to handle their shipbuilding contracts. The ship manufacturers built homes to accommodate the influx of people coming in. Most of the shipbuilders' black employees were offered housing on Flower Hill as a recruiting incentive, although they still had to pay rent. Quonset huts were used primarily during World War II to house military men where they were stationed. A large surplus of these Quonset huts existed and could be purchased very cheaply by private companies. In addition, the huts were easy to assemble and were modified to house at least two families per unit.

Later, the manufacturers in Chester had contractors build brick townhomes and offer them at much higher lease prices. I remembered, as Judy was talking, that we had lived in one of those quonset places when we first came to the township. On the drive to Flower Hill, Judy invited me to come to her house the following Sunday. She asked me to get permission from my mother and father. She said her son would pick me up. She dropped me off at my front door and apologized again for what that store owner had said.

That night I felt so good, because Judy had made me feel valuable. I remember what my father and mother said when I explained to them what had happened that day. My mother said, "See, that's why you can't judge people by their color."

My father was more concerned about my safety but relaxed when I told him Judy said she was going to have her husband talk to the man. Then my father said, "Black people are coming to the point when we will bow no more to white people."

When I had dinner the following Sunday with my employer's family, they treated me in such an apologetic manner, and it made me feel good. The family spoke of the racial injustices they felt should not exist in America. Judy's son and daughter were adamant that change would come in time. They even requested their African American maid and cook sit at the dinner table with us. The maid told me later that she sat with the family for dinner on many occasions, when time permitted. She wanted me to know the family was genuine. After that night, I began to realize the importance of white people taking a stance against the institutional racism and unequal laws existing in America.

To my chagrin, Judy sold that retail store during the following school year, and I was not reemployed by the new owners. I had no contact with the family after the sale of the store; however, when their housemaid would see me in the neighborhood, she always said they wanted me to come back to visit someday.

I realized how significant my father's statement about bowing was much later in life. In 2004, during a family reunion in Hawaii, my youngest brother and I began a discussion about how our father's behavior changed noticeably in the presence of white men. My father would bow noticeably and say "Yes, sir" to the white man. He would smile frequently and physically tremble in the presence of a white man. His body language was that of a subservient rather than that of a free man. We agreed that his behavior was probably a survival technique he used growing up under oppressive Caucasians in Mississippi—a replica of Harriet Beecher Stowe's Uncle Tom character.

That behavior from African Americans (yessir boss) illuminated the only relationship that was acceptable between them and Southern Caucasians during that era. During our conversation in 2004, I also revealed to my youngest brother a statement our father had made back in 1957. As my father and I watched the news about the Little Rock Nine who were attempting to desegregate the "white only" high school in Little Rock, Arkansas, my father made a profound statement. We watched the throngs of white people displaying their hatred as the Little Rock Nine entered the school, and our father said, "I have been bowing to white people all my life. I hope your generation will make it so that we as colored people will have to bow no more." My father made statements to me about not bowing to the white man often. It was something about which he obviously felt very strongly.

8

Desegregation

The next three summers, I was employed doing construction work, helping to build residential homes. A neighborhood acquaintance of my father, a roofer, got the foreman to hire me and his son as apprentice helpers for the construction company. Later, I spent a portion of my summer, after my high school graduation, living with old neighborhood friends who had moved from Chester and working as a dishwasher at a posh restaurant in the Philadelphia suburbs. The thing I remember most about that restaurant experience was how the reception employees there would tell African American customers that the restaurant was booked full, even if they had called in a reservation. I knew they were lying on many occasions. One of the chefs there simply told me, "If customers saw the restaurant serving colored people, it would hurt the business." His statement felt like a deliberate jab at me. But I controlled my anger and let it go, without comment.

Graduating from Chester Township's Perry Wright Elementary School and going into the ninth grade at Douglas Junior High School was another elevating experience into the real world. The junior high school was about a mile walk from Flower Hill. The territory that was Flower Street down to the Delaware River and bordered by Engle Street actually represented the unspoken racial segregation from the rest of Chester. It was the accepted norm during that period. While attending Douglas Junior High School, I learned that any references to African American history or injustices to African Americans were taboo subjects—just as it had been at Perry Wright Elementary School. The teachers at both schools were African Americans, and they did not encourage any discussion about racial issues. There was no subject concerning racial issues in any of the curriculum.

Near graduation from Douglas Junior High School, a course preference document for entry into Chester High School was issued to each graduating student. I chose the vocational course that Chester High School was offering, mainly because I had enjoyed working with that construction contractor during the summer months. At fifteen, my first intermingling contact with white kids my age came with entry into Chester High School. Chester High School was located a few miles away, which meant we had to catch a bus each morning to get to school. The bus tickets were paid for by the local school district. The bus route wove through the white part of Chester Township before it got to our stop on Engle Street. The first time I got on the bus to go to high school, I was waiting with five other people to get on the bus. I was the last one to board the bus, and after I deposited my ticket and turned to sit down, I noticed that all of the African American kids went to the back of the bus. At that moment, I suddenly remembered Mrs. Rosa Parks, who refused to sit in the back of the bus in Alabama and sparked a civil rights revolution. I sat down in the second row instead of going to the rear. I sat next to a white girl, whom I found out later would be a classmate in one of my classes.

Getting off the bus and walking into Chester High School for the first time was a bit of a shocking realization for me. For the first time in my life, I was in the midst of a sea of white faces. I found out later that the African American to white ratio of the 2,100 people attending classes each semester was about even. I felt self-conscious when I first walked into the lobby. There were a few stares at the large group of African Americans suddenly standing in the lobby, but nothing like I was afraid it was going to be. It was an exciting first day. I especially enjoyed meeting my Caucasian classmates. Most of my white classmates had attended ninth grade at Chester High School and were familiar with the high school routines. In homeroom, my classmates made us feel welcome. The new township attendees were split up to different homerooms to accommodate our numbers. That morning, for the first time in my young life, I felt I was accepted as an American. As time went on, however, I learned that this feeling of acceptance would be tarnished by individual racial prejudices, social injustices, and legal injustices that were underlined by institutional racism. There were experiences at Chester High School that hurt me deeply.

During my sophomore year, one of my classmates, Gary, who was of Italian descent, and I became good friends. Our friendship had been limited to school time. We were both enrolled in the vocational maintenance course and attended the same English, history, math, and physics classes. We both enjoyed rock and roll music. He invited me to go with him to a nearby restaurant, which was a hangout for teenagers during the lunch hour and had a jukebox that played rock and roll. I had never been there. When I entered the restaurant, I noticed right away that I was the only African American in the restaurant. There were a lot of stares as we found an empty booth. When a waitress came to the booth to take our order, she not once acknowledged my presence and spoke only to my friend. Gary had to ask me what I wanted to eat and relayed that to the waitress. While Gary and I were eating, one of the guys came over to our booth and asked Gary if he could speak to him in private. When he came back to the booth, I could feel something wasn't right. We didn't talk, and he kept encouraging me to eat faster so we could leave the restaurant. He was still quiet as we walked to our next class. We were early, and while we were the only ones present at the time, I asked him what the problem was. He said that a couple of guys told him it was not a good thing to bring a colored person into the restaurant. He then apologized for what happened, and he vowed never to go there again.

While riding the bus to the township after classes, I felt the hurt but buried it deep inside. What was really oxymoronic to me was that most of the rock and roll music the people in the

29

restaurant was listening to was played by African American musicians and singers. The next day, Gary invited me to his home, which was located about two blocks from the high school, for a pasta lunch. I was hesitant to accept the invitation at first and asked him if he was sure, because of what happened the day before. He assured me there was no problem, and we enjoyed a beautiful lunch that his mother had warmed up for us. His mother's English was not that good, but the conversation was still pleasant. She enjoyed us coming to the house for lunch, and we did that for the rest of the school year. Mother Annie urged me to give my friend's mother my lunch allowance, since she was feeding me every day. I told my friend what my mother wanted me to do, and he said no, to do that would hurt her feelings. The pain of that rejection at the restaurant was slowly disappearing with time. Gary and I remained friends throughout our Chester High School tenure. We both enlisted in the U.S. Navy after graduation and attended the same boot camp. We got together a couple times in 1965 while I was between service enlistments. I got a chance to visit his mother again in 1965, and his family really made me feel like it was my home. The last time I saw Gary was at the U.S. Navy Seabee Base enlisted men's club at Da Nang, Vietnam. I learned the next week that he had been killed while on patrol in the jungles of Vietnam.

The young teenage white girl, Jane, who I sat next to on my first high school bus run happened to be my classmate in American history. We recognized each other in that first class as township "neighbors." We chatted a lot on the next bus trip. Jane would put her school books on the seat next to her to save the seat for me. I began to notice on that bus ride the stares from other whites and the African Americans on the bus that we were sitting together. She was not that fluent in English. Jane and her family had recently emigrated from Poland. I did not see her on the bus at the end of the day because her school activities lasted longer than mine. Jane and I began discussing American history. I was explaining a lot of American history to her to help her with the weekly exams. Jane once asked me why there was no African American history in American history books. I could not answer that question, except to tell her of some of the existing social and educational prejudices. I did say that someday—once society changed—the history books would document the history of African Americans.

Jane and I really enjoyed each other's company and our history discussions during those school bus rides. Then one day, just after the Thanksgiving holiday break, I noticed that Jane started to get very quiet on the bus. She also stopped saving the seat next to her. I kept going over in my mind whether I did or said something that offended her. Even in the classroom, Jane would ignore me when I said hello. Then one day, when the high school was closed during the Christmas holiday, I saw Jane in downtown Chester. I stopped and said hello to her, and she had a perplexed look on her face. She then suggested that we go to a nearby park to talk. The park was a short walking distance, and I tried to make conversation with her about the Christmas holiday on the way. She did not say much in response. When we got to the park bench and sat down, I asked her if something was wrong. When she turned to face me, there were tears in her eyes. We were both fifteen years old.

Jane explained to me that during the Thanksgiving holiday, her parents told her to stop associating with me. She said one of her girlfriend's parents had told her parents that we would sit and talk with each other. Her parents told her it was very wrong to associate with a colored boy in America. She told me that she felt very hurt by what they said. She said, "It's not right. You're my friend."

I felt like I had just been stabbed with a knife. I told her not to cry, that someday things would change in America. I said, "Someday maybe you and I will help change things." Jane and I went our separate ways that day. We spoke to each other the rest of our high school term only to say hello. I do remember that as we congratulated each other after the Chester High School graduation ceremonies, Jane turned to me and said, "Let's go change things." I was pleased that she had remembered me saying that so long ago.

Well, Jane certainly did her part. In 1962, when I returned home on leave during my enlistment with the U.S. Navy, I found out she was involved with Freedom Riders, a group of black and white students who would travel through the South and participate in lunch counter sit-ins. Segregation in Southern states stated that, by law, stores could not serve African Americans at the eating facilities. Jane was a student at a nearby university at the time. I felt very proud of her when I saw her interview on television. I remember saying to myself, "Make them pay for your tears!"

9

Annie: The Mother

Another tremendous experience during high school involved Mother Annie. The history teacher requested that each student bring in a short essay on a historical event in American history. It was 1958, and the civil rights revolution was beginning. I was contemplating what I would bring in for that Friday's essay presentation. The news programs were concentrating on the ongoing civil disobedience occurring in the Southern portions of the United States. African Americans were marching through cities of the South, crying out for social and legal justice, while whites in those same areas were spitting their wrath at those brave people. I decided one night, after a lot of thought, what I was going to do. The next day, after school, I picked up two magazines with which I was familiar, *Ebony* and *Jet*, and began reading. I decided that an editorial piece was the best description of my inner anger. I copied the narrative, word for word, and took it to class for my Friday essay exam.

When my turn came on Friday to read my historical essay, I stood with pride to read. As I was reading the essay and glancing about the room, I could see that most of the white faces were bowed as I read. The article was an attack on American racism and American society for allowing social and legal injustices toward African Americans to exist. The reading of the essay only took about ten minutes. As I was reading, I noticed the history teacher's face was turning red. When I finished reading, the teacher dismissed the class, even though we had about ten minutes left until the bell rang. As I was leaving, I noticed my Polish friend, Jane, staring at me and smiling. Jane looked at me and said, "That was good. Thank you, Hollis." She said that right in front of the history teacher, who was still seated at his desk.

As I left the room, I could tell the teacher was still angry. As I was walking down the hallway, I could see people from my history class staring at me from their lockers. By the time I got on the bus to go home, I felt like I had committed some kind of crime. There were no derogatory comments from other students on the bus, just stares. Even my African American schoolmates stared at me. I did not relay what had happened in my history class to my parents that night, afraid I would arouse their ire for doing such a thing. When I got to my homeroom class the following Monday morning and after the homeroom class teacher dismissed us to begin classes, he asked me to stay behind to speak to me. He told me to report to the vice principal's office.

When I got to the vice principal's office, after waiting for about ten minutes, the vice principal's secretary motioned for me to go into his office. The secretary followed me into the office and sat down as I stood in front of the vice principal's desk. The vice principal began the conversation with queries into my family life and my family's history. After awhile, he asked me why I had made those racial statements in my American history class. I pretended not to know what he meant, but I knew. I explained to him that the history teacher had instructed that everyone in the class read a short essay of American history. I told him that because it was American history I chose to bring in writings about social and legal injustices endured by African Americans since the end of the Civil War. The vice principal told me that the subject was not appropriate for high school and that I was viewed as a troublemaker. He then informed me that I would be suspended from school for three days and that a parent had to accompany me back to school that following Friday. He told me to clear out my locker and to leave that morning, and I obeyed.

When I got home, I pretended to be sick to explain my early arrival from school. That night during dinner, I explained to my mother and father that I really had felt sick when I got home, but it was because of what happened that day. After I explained to them what happened and why I was suspended from school, they were shocked by the reason for the suspension. Mother Annie was livid. My father remained silent. My father only stated that he would not be able to go to the school with us on Friday because of his job. After Mom had calmed down a bit, she asked to see the essay I read to the class. After reading the essay, Mother's first comment was, "These people don't want to face the truth." Mother Annie made no comment about the situation the rest of the night, but each time I looked at her, her face was flushed. Mom and I took the bus to Chester High School that Friday morning. She seemed very calm and even joked with some of the people that she knew who were on the bus.

When we entered the vice principal's office, Mother Annie seemed very in control of her demeanor. She calmly told the secretary her name and asked to see the vice principal. The secretary went into the vice principal's office to inform him we were there. When we stepped into his office and took the seats that were offered us, I felt like I had caused a lot of trouble. The vice principal held out his hand toward me. "What the essay does is cause friction between the black and white students. And the parents of some of the white students are complaining that you read something so controversial in class. They're even planning on going to the school board. I can't have that happen." He finished by saying, "I hope you understand the problem with Hollis reading this type of essay."

Mother Annie calmly asked him, "Was Hollis told that there was a restriction concerning what type of essay he could give?"

The vice principal said he would have to check on that before he could answer that question.

She then said, "If my son was not given any restrictions on the essay, then I must say that your teacher and your school have violated his constitutional right to free speech." Mother Annie continued, "If you insist on any further punishment of my child concerning his essay, I will contact the NAACP and the National Urban League lawyers to monitor this situation." I had a little knowledge about the existence of the NAACP and the National Urban League and could sense the value of these organizations more prominently the moment she said those words.

The vice principal looked stunned. He said, "We don't wish to have any legal problems over this." Then he went on to explain that this kind of essay could cause racial problems with the classmates in the school.

My mother countered that if there were restrictions on speech in the classroom, then it should be identified in a manner consistent with the board of education instructions. The vice principal and the secretary were very subdued by my mother's statements. I was shocked because I had never heard her articulate her feelings with such fortitude. The vice principal thanked Mother Annie for coming in and instructed me to resume my classes on the following Monday. I felt so proud of Mom as we walked down the hallway and out of the school. On the way home, Mom and I talked about the two organizations she had mentioned, and she educated me more about their function. She also made me promise I would let her read any material that had to do with racial issues before taking it to class. I promised her, but I also promised myself I would never bring up racial issues in school again.

I did not learn for years later that Mother Annie had spoken to lawyers from the NAACP and the Urban League about how to handle my suspension from school. The lawyers had told her exactly what to say to the vice principal!

10

The Basketball Pain

Another painful saga occurred during the high school basketball season of my senior year. At that time, Chester High School's basketball team was one of the top teams in the Pennsylvania Interscholastic Athletic Association. (PIAA). One of the state championship games, which included Chester High School and a western Pennsylvania high school, was played in an enclosed stadium in Philadelphia. I attended the game, and seated in the upper level, I noticed a group of people with signs that were derogatory toward African Americans. The signs read "Beat the nigs" and "Apes can jump higher." The sign that really hurt my feelings read "Go back to Africa."

At that particular time, the Chester High School basketball team was comprised mostly of African American players. I didn't know why that particular sign bothered me so much. I can only surmise that it was because Africa was considered a very primitive continent, even by African American people. In the end, Chester High School lost a close and exciting game. Leaving the stadium, I was stopped by some of my high school peers, who were angry about the signs. I told one of them to let it go, and he said no. I stopped an African American security guard who was walking by us and asked if anything could be done to stop people from bringing derogatory signs like that to a game. The security guard shrugged and said, "No, because it was freedom of speech in a public setting." As we were leaving the stadium, a brawl began, which could easily be seen as a racial conflict. Two people were almost beaten to death, and several other people ended up in the hospital from injuries sustained during the melee. I decided not to get involved with this violence. My rationale came from what my parents had taught me—that violence is not the answer.

The next day, I learned that it was only the Chester High School African American students who got involved in the melee with students from the other school. It bothered me that none of my white peers were involved in the fracas. It felt as if my white classmates were condoning the behavior of the people yelling racial slurs and cheering for the opposing team.

But my opinion soon changed. The Chester High School principal called an emergency session in the gymnasium for all students. We were all gathered in the stands. The principal came down hard on all of us for behavior that tarnished the reputation of a great high school. I agreed that this brawl should never have happened. The principal spoke in terms of "we" and "us." The principal's words were so profound that there were tears shed by many students, including me. The vice principal's daughter was seated next to me, and I remember her saying to a friend, "We really messed up, getting into a fight like that." It impressed me to hear her say that, mostly because she used the word *we*. The brawl was started by African American students in a rage about those signs. But the attitude about the event was that it affected all the students. I felt a sense of pride that my classmates viewed the antagonism from the other school as a "we" thing. That the people cheering for the other school's basketball team ridiculed all of us and not just the African American students supporting the Chester High School team. I graduated from Chester High School later that year with a deeper resolve that people cannot be judged by their race but the content of their character.

PART TWO
The Journey Begins

1

Recruitment

In my generation, African Americans were a rarity in specialized occupations in the U.S. Navy. I eventually became a U.S. Navy Seabee (Construction Battalions). I was in the midst of a historic transformation within the U.S. Navy. When the Navy recruiter visited Chester High School in 1959 and mentioned the opportunity to get construction experience, I was surprised. I had never thought of the U.S. Navy in terms of construction. I had worked three straight summers in construction and had learned everything from carpentry to roofing. Chester High School had a good vocational studies program where I had learned additional skills, from millwork to building maintenance, which included electrical and plumbing maintenance. My parents had considered college for me, but finances were an obstacle. The Navy looked like a good bet, and the chance to go into construction made the decision easy. I signed up and checked the box for the U.S. Navy construction occupational rating.

In 1848, President Harry Truman had signed into law a bill that desegregated the armed forces of the United States. What I didn't know when I signed up was that African Americans in my era were seldom recruited into specialized occupational billets in the U.S. Navy. Instead, African Americans were offered mostly menial job ratings, such as stewards or cooks. To this day I'm not sure how my enlistment paperwork slipped through the U.S. Navy recruiters screening process. It could be because I attended a racially integrated high school. My paperwork was approved in a letter sent to my parents, and the letter showed my approval for the construction rating. The letter also acknowledged that I had to be eighteen years old to qualify. So Mother Annie sent them a copy of my social security paperwork, which showed my birth date and current address. I got the approval paperwork in the mail and was told to report to the recruiting office.

When I walked into the recruiting office with the approval paperwork, the recruiter reading the paperwork looked shocked. One recruiter in that office even tried to talk me out of becoming a Seabee. But I had my approval paperwork, and the recruiters were bound by that approval signature. On September 17, 1959, I enlisted in the U.S. Navy.

2

Boot Camp

Boot camp was a brutal realization to an eighteen-year-old. Boot camp made the whole world as I knew it almost nonexistent—with one exception in my case—racist cruelty. I was the only African American in my boot camp company, and after only two days, I was crying inside to be with Mother Annie again.

I remember leaving her to walk into downtown Chester to the recruiting station for departure to boot camp. I felt that same feeling that I had the day she took me to elementary school. I remember saying good-bye to her, and I took off walking. I wanted to run back to her. I knew she was still watching me from the screen door, and I turned to look at her at the last moment when I knew I would be out of sight. She was still standing in the doorway watching. And then I could see her no more. My heart was in pain as I thought about this journey I was taking.

I took a flight from Philadelphia to Chicago and a bus to the U.S. Navy boot camp located in Waukegan, Illinois. Being the only African American in my boot camp training company was a deeply emotional experience for me. I was determined to succeed no matter how much they tortured me. I could understand all the marching, physical fitness training, standing watch, barracks cleaning and inspections, classroom training, uniform inspections, and ridicule from our leader. But I had to withstand more. Being called "nigger boy" in my face by the petty officer in charge was the most challenging. Someone pasted a picture of a gorilla on my locker with the words "Go back to Africa" written on it. I would come back from taking a shower and find the spit shine on my boots, which I had prepared for the next day's inspection, completely ruined. Someone squirted lighter fluid on my bed sheets once. One night, I was standing a four-hour watch, outside in zero-degree weather next to a dumpster, and was not relieved until six hours had passed. Still I said nothing.

I realized early on that my company mates were watching me, even whispering about me, but I refused to let them see that I was suffering. When I would sit at the large recreation table in the middle of the barracks floor, the guys already seated would leave. Nobody would sit at the table with me. One night, when I returned from standing a watch, a piece of cloth was laid on my bunk bed with eyes and a mouth cut out. It was the Ku Klux Klan symbol. I tore it up and threw it in the trash can, near where the guys were seated at the recreational table. As I returned to my bunk bed, I could hear the guys laughing. I lay there angry but kept telling myself not to say anything.

One Sunday, after returning from the chow hall, where I had sat alone, I decided to read the newspaper we were allowed to take to the barracks. As I lay in bed reading, my bunkmate who slept above me looked down at me and asked if we could talk. He asked why I didn't just quit the Navy instead of taking all the crap—his words—that was being thrown at me. I responded, "Because I want to be a Navy Seabee. I will not quit."

Then he told me that after that Ku Klux Klan incident he got called into the office of the chief in charge of the company, who had heard about the incident. He then relayed that the chief in charge had told him to tell me to hang in there and that he would resolve the problems I was having. And in a short period of time, change did happen. I found out later that the chief in charge had a meeting with my company mates while I was standing watch. The whole environment seemed to change. I experienced no more harassment. I learned later the root of the harassment had been two guys in the company from South Carolina who kept stirring up racist sentiments. Soon they were gone from the company, transferred to another company that had no African American recruits. My whole existence at boot camp became more bearable.

When I returned home after the three months of training, I realized that boot camp had opened the door to manhood. While I was in boot camp, my father and mother managed to buy a home in the suburbs of Philadelphia, a place named Sharon Hill, Pennsylvania. When I returned home, I could see my mom as a person, not only a mother. Later in life, I realized that Mother Annie would always live inside me.

PART THREE
Military Time

1

Seabees

I moved on to a rewarding twenty-three-year career as a U.S. Navy Seabee. The name "Seabee" was adapted from the initials for Construction Battalions, which were formed during World War II as support units for landing armed forces. "We Build, We Fight" is the Seabee motto. Being able to say I served with these elite units is one of the greatest satisfactions of my life.

My journey through this rewarding career, however, was not an easy one. I am not sure I was the first African American Seabee, but I was certainly among the first, and I bore the brunt of the racist attitude that was ubiquitous in the armed forces in those years. But I was also privileged to be a part of the momentous and historic changes that transformed the U.S. Navy into a fighting force that is truly American, harnessing the energies, skills, and patriotism of all its citizens, regardless of their race.

Racist attitudes were present right from the start at Seabee construction school in Port Hueneme, California, where I spent three months in the utilities man training. Countless daily incidents—mostly small, some big—made it clear that I was considered to be less a person than the others.

On my first day in the mess hall, I lined up to eat with everyone else. When I got to the head, a galley monitor stopped me. "The chief wants you to stand by a minute," he said. So I backed out of the line and stood by. After everyone had passed through the line, he motioned for me to go ahead. I picked up my meal and walked to the table where some of the utilities man trainees from my class were sitting. I sat down. They all stood up and moved to another table. I lost my appetite when I realized what was going on. I walked out of the mess hall before finishing the meal. I walked back to the classroom with a really heavy heart. Even so, I felt a determination that I would not let these behaviors defeat me.

A lot of the behavior seemed intended to wear me down: Sambo drawings left on my desk and "nigger" written on my desk or my locker. And it wasn't just classmates displaying this racist attitude. Much of the racism came from the top down, from older guys who had been in the Navy for years. I always got the most menial and dirty tasks, such as cleaning the bathrooms. Despite all that, the person-to-person environment did slowly improve. People's individual reactions to my presence varied, from hostility to friendship. It helped that I am outgoing—that I have an avid interest in people and that my parents taught me not to harbor racial prejudice.

Before I left utilities man school, one of my instructors told me he admired my attitude and fortitude in dealing with the racism. I felt pretty good about his statement. It seemed that I was helping in a small way to address American racism one-on-one. I finally managed to graduate from the school and was given the utilities man apprentice rating. After the graduation ceremony, one white chief petty officer told me that he was happy I did not quit the course. He stated that he hoped someday that the "racist crap" he saw me endure would not be part of the U.S. Navy. It was good to know that there were people who regretted racist behaviors. And I began to realize that an end to racism in the U.S. Navy would have to begin at the top of leadership.

After graduation, I received orders to report to U.S. Naval Station Midway Island, located in the Pacific Ocean in the Hawaiian Island chain. Midway is an island about two miles wide by a mile long and is very isolated. I spent about five days on Oahu, Hawaii, while awaiting transportation to Midway Island. Hawaii's culture impressed me deeply. Hawaii is a melting pot of diverse cultures and races that displays the human connection in a very special way. A wonderful friendliness pervades the island people. The island families include Native Hawaiians, Chinese, Japanese, Koreans, Pacific Islanders, and Filipinos. Caucasian people—or "haoles" as referred to in the Native Hawaiian tongue—are actually in the minority of the Hawaii population. I spent those five days cruising around Oahu in a rental car with some haole U.S. Navy guys who were also going to Midway Island. We met at the military barracks. I never felt the stigma of being an African American during those five days in Hawaii with all its blended cultures.

Midway Island was desolate for my young, eighteen-year-old mind. I spent one year, two days, and four hours on Midway Island. My duties included the following: drinking water pumping station attendant, power house boiler watch, and after-hours utilities shop emergency response. I advanced two pay grades while on Midway Island. We had some racial problems, and most happened at the enlisted men's club. When some of the white guys got to drinking, racist words slipped out, and there was animosity. The enlisted men's club on Midway Island was where I saw for the first time since coming into the military a lot of African Americans gather in one place. Many were relegated to menial ratings within the U.S. Navy, such as stewards and cooks. I did notice two African American guys in specialized aviation ratings.

Once I was pulled aside by one of the African American guys and asked why I only sat with white guys whenever I came to the enlisted men's club. I explained that they were the guys I worked with every day and that I didn't mean to slight anyone. The next time I went back to the club, I sat with the African American guys. After several nights, I was approached by one of my co-workers, who asked why I didn't sit with them at the club anymore. I explained to him the dilemma. I did try once to get a couple African American guys to sit at the table with me and my co-workers, but they were not interested. I felt so confused and kept asking myself why people felt so separated. Deep inside I knew the answer. I could see that the prevailing social ills and prejudices between the races in American society was also a part of the U.S. Navy culture. After that, I refrained from going to the enlisted men's club again.

After my tour of duty at Naval Station Midway Island, I was assigned to Naval Mobile Construction Battalion Three (NMCB-3), home ported at Port Hueneme, California. We later deployed to Okinawa, Japan. This was nearly sixteen years after World War II ended, and Okinawa was still under the sovereignty of the United States. This assignment was where I really felt like a Seabee. I was enjoying teamwork in its best form and sharpening my skills by concentrating on daily construction activities. I still believe that working together in an intense, goal-oriented environment is one of the most effective antidotes to racism over the long-term. On the job, your skills are needed, your expertise is valued, and your manual labor is as critical as the person's working next to you. Prejudice is more likely to sit in the back of the bus.

2

Where's Your Tail?

Just being in a Construction Battalion unit did not end racism. I was reminded that I was African American in many ways. For example, at the construction jobsite where we worked, we had what was called a Lister bag, which contained water for us to drink when the water wagon was elsewhere or being filled. The Lister bag had a metal cup attached. One time, I walked over to use the cup attached, but before I could pick it up, the chief petty officer came over and said, "Hang on, son, hang on." Then he called out, "Anybody else need to use the cup?" Some of my co-workers came over and stood in line to use the cup. Only after they all had used the cup was I allowed to take a drink. This action was done in a low-key, almost friendly way—as if the black person in the crew was a second-class citizen.

For African American sailors on liberty in Okinawa, an amazing Jim Crow–style segregation prevailed. African Americans went to the bars and restaurants in the district called Koza City. Show up anywhere else, and the military police (MPs) would run you away. One time, early in our deployment to Okinawa, I, along with another African American guy, mistakenly entered a bar that was frequented by white military servicemen. A couple of bar girls approached us. One of the girls kept looking behind me, staring at my back, and touching me, chattering to her friend in Okinawa language, which is considered separate from Japanese.

"What are you doing?" I asked her.

She replied that the white guys had told her that black people had tails, and she wanted to see if that were true. She was serious!

"No way," I said. "You don't feel anything back there, do you?"

About that time a couple of white guys came in the door. "You're not supposed to be in here," one of them said. To avoid trouble, we left that bar. It was months later, when I was in Koza City at one of the bars, that I saw one of those same girls working as a cashier. We joked about what had happened, and she assured me that she had been really serious at the time. When she grew up, the American whites were like rulers, after seizing Okinawa during World War II. Anything the white people said was true in her mind.

That deployment was where I saw the fabled "ugly American." As an African American, it was distressing to witness the overall American racial attitude toward the Japanese people. Local Okinawa U.S. civil service employees were underpaid and bullied; Okinawa women were exploited. The Okinawa culture was openly ridiculed, and drunken assaults against Okinawa people were common. Granted, this was 1961—just sixteen years after the end of a terrible war. And it was clear that the average American serviceman did not look upon the Japanese as human. As an African American, I could relate. But most disturbing was that at the time there were no orders from high-ranking American officials countervailing the mistreatment of local Okinawa people.

It was my experience that African Americans bore the brunt of the discriminatory attitudes that were rampant in the armed forces in those years. Even though President Truman had integrated the armed forces in 1948, attitudes were very slow to change.

3

Subic Bay, Philippines

After my deployment with NMCB-3, I was assigned to the U.S. Naval Station Subic Bay, Philippines. I was assigned to work at the Public Works Center fuel supply depot. Professionally, this was an interesting assignment. My duties included delivering bulk fuel to U.S. Navy ships—namely, destroyers, aircraft carriers, and cruisers. I also learned a lot about fuel oil storage, fuel testing, and firefighting. I enjoyed the Filipino culture immensely. And in the Philippines I did not feel the horrible sting of pervasive racism.

While I was in the Philippines, my first U.S. Navy Seabee enlistment was approaching its end. I had attained the rank of E-5 by this time, and naval station recruiters began soliciting me to reenlist. I was torn emotionally. The work of a Seabee was extraordinarily rewarding, and I had matured and learned much from the Seabee experience. I had risen to the point where I was instructing others and supervising crews. But the racist attitudes among my white peers and seniors, coupled with my feeling that nothing was being done to change them, wore me down. In addition, there was no indication for upward advancement. I had risen to second class petty officer. I seldom saw an African American in the Navy at the first class rank, unless it was in a menial rating. It was the same with chief petty officers. And except for chaplains, I never did observe an African American commissioned officer in the U.S. Navy during my entire enlistment. And the truth was, I had no inward desire to reenlist. In September 1963, I was released to inactive duty from the U.S. Navy.

Part Four
The Journey Back

1

Civilian Life

Upon return to civilian life, Annie's child felt a sense of relief from the years of conformity. At age twenty-two, I felt a sense of freedom and embarked on the next phase of my new adulthood. The next few years would bring a maelstrom of events into my life and to the United States.

In the civilian world, the racial climate was very bad. In those years, an African American with construction experience, no matter the educational certification in his background, was immediately relegated to an apprentice or an apprentice helper— the same type of employment duties I had during those summers while in high school. Most African Americans in construction had to hold the apprentice position for many years before attaining any type of certification. The pay level in the apprentice position was not very good. I began looking for other employment, based on my education and training. But my search for employment was interrupted by a great American tragedy.

On November 22, 1963, after returning home from a job interview, my brother Brook telephoned me. He said, "Turn on the television. You're not going to believe this. The president has been shot."

I didn't comprehend what Brook was saying. I was thinking, "What president?" There was no way I could imagine it being the president of the United States. But it was. It was the president of the United States, John Kennedy, who had been killed by a sniper's bullet!

When that famous newscaster, the late Walter Cronkite, said the words, "The president of the United States, John Kennedy, is dead," my heart felt like it had sunk to my knees. I felt sickened by this tragedy! "What's next?" I thought. "Are we going to be invaded by another country?" People from all walks of life mourned in shock that weekend. Here was a young president who had given hope for a better America to millions during his new presidency. In trying to provide equal rights and equal justice for African Americans, he had taken huge leaps. African Americans turned to embrace President Kennedy and his administration in the fight for civil rights. The president's assassination was a tragedy that was a monumental part of civil, judicial, and social unrest in American society.

In an effort to recover emotionally from the assassination tragedy, I continued my quest to build a future in the civilian world. I had started collecting unemployment insurance in October of that year and began a weekly trek to different companies seeking employment.

2

Post-Military Employment

The employment office had me do an interview that December with an auto parts distributor located near my home in Lansdowne, Pennsylvania. I started working for the auto parts distributor in January 1964. After two weeks, I noticed that I had not yet been assigned as an auto parts desk clerk, which had been identified in my application form as my employment position. I was doing mostly warehouse stocking. I understood this in the beginning—I needed to learn the basics of the business. But after a month working in the warehouse, I began to ask questions. I was the only African American working for that company at the time.

I later found out why I wasn't given the position for which I was hired after a lengthy conversation with the supervisor of the warehouse division of the auto parts company. After my continual questioning of the two clerks working at the sales desk, I discovered one clerk had been hired after I started working in the stocking area of the warehouse. I was upset. Why had someone else been hired to take the position I had been hired to work? I demanded to talk to the supervisor. He was honest with me and told me that I was hired to accommodate the parent company's new policy to hire minorities. I then asked why I was not working in the position I was hired to work.

The supervisor told me, "It's not a good image for the sales department to have a Negro guy at the sales counter." I asked him why, and he said, "Don't get me wrong, but most white people don't think colored people are that smart." His statement made me feel like I had been punched in the chest. I maintained my cool, although I was seething inside. I then asked why they had hired me under that job title.

The supervisor said that his office was under pressure from the corporation to hire an African American right away. The NAACP and the local Urban League had been putting pressure on the company—with the threat of legal action—if their compliance requests were not met within a certain time period. He stated that my job title was the only opening they had at the time. So they had filled the position with me after getting the pertinent information from the unemployment office personnel. After I was hired, a warehouse position actually opened up, so they kept me there and hired another person in the clerk position. He stated that the company was in the process of changing my employment title to warehouseman. The man spoke politely about the situation. He stated that he thought I was a very good worker and very reliable. He stated that someday he would make sure I advanced to a better-paying position.

I left him with the impression that I agreed with the situation, but I was burning inside. I noticed later that afternoon that the three other warehousemen were watching every move I made. Perhaps they were worried I might do some damage to their property. I kept smiling and joking and adopted that "Yawsa boss" demeanor for the rest of the day. It was Friday, and I had the weekend to think about what had happened. I felt so hurt inside. I didn't mind being a token; I had gone through that in the military. It was his statement that most white people didn't think that colored people were that smart that hurt me the most. Walking home that afternoon, I kept remembering my father's statement about my generation providing the change so that African Americans would bow no more.

That Saturday, I attended a local high school basketball game with an African American friend. I had remembered that the local chapter of the National Urban League had written an article in their local newsletter about me while I had been stationed in the Philippines. The article was mainly recognition that I had joined the U.S. Navy's elite, specialized Seabees. I spoke to my friend about my dilemma on the job and asked if he knew anyone associated with the National Urban League. Luckily, he had a neighbor whose father was a member of the Philadelphia National Urban League. His name was John. My friend arranged for me to go to John's house to speak to him the next day—Sunday.

I told John, the Urban League member, exactly what the supervisor at the automobile parts company stated to me. John shrugged. "It's their way of complying with the orders of the corporation of hiring by a certain deadline. What I want you to do is to go back to work on Monday. Tell me about your work experience."

I gave him the details of my military career and teenage employment experience.

John nodded. "Make sure you have a copy of your DD214 military discharge certificate and high school records on hand." I was puzzled as to why he wanted me to have these documents available. John said, "I'll be in contact with you later in the week with a resolution about this hiring problem."

I went to work as usual on Monday, stocking and moving parts. On Wednesday evening, I got a call from the Philadelphia National Urban League Office. They asked me to come to the office the following Saturday to discuss my employment issue. John also called to confirm that I got the message from the Philadelphia office. I thanked him and told him yes. He wished me luck. I was still a bit confused on how they were going to handle the problem. If they could somehow force my employer to put me in the clerk position, I knew it would create a hostile work environment. But I felt determined that I should not be treated like a token. I had already endured enough racism in my life. It was time to bow no more.

On Saturday, I met with the National Urban League staffer who handled employment issues for the Philadelphia area. He told me that through a legal loophole the company I worked for could not be forced to put me in that parts desk clerk position. He did, however, offered me a guaranteed position with a Philadelphia Westinghouse Electric Company. The staffer went on to explain to me that companies were feeling the pressure to hire minorities, and that's why the position as an electric motor repair winder was available at Westinghouse Electric. He explained that he was telling me this because he suspected a hostile environment for me with the co-workers at my present place of employment. I jumped at the opportunity. This type of job was in line with my previous training and experience, and it paid much more. The staffer said my background seemed to fit the position. He had me fill out a formal resume for submission and approved me for hire in that position. He explained there would be a three-month probation period. He also said I had to give my current employer two weeks' notice of resignation, in writing, with a copy going to him at the Philadelphia National Urban League Office. I gave the auto parts company a two-week notice, and they let me go a week earlier, with pay. I found out much later that they had hired a new African American warehouseman a week after I left the position.

Working at the Westinghouse Division in Philadelphia was hassle free. I encountered no overt racist attitudes. After three months' employment, I was required to join the union. The International Brotherhood of Electrical Workers Union (IBEW) was good about resolving worker complaints and other issues that needed to be rectified by the management. After two years with Westinghouse, I accepted an offer for employment with General Electric. General Electric had the same IBEW union. During my tenure with General Electric, the IBEW union did go on strike once, for four days. I participated in the strike, which concerned promotion and equal pay for black employees in comparison to white employees. The strike involved the company on a national scale.

3

Change

Early in the 1960s, there were racially motivated events occurring within the United States that would affect American history so much that the events would later be known as a revolution.

For instance, just before I left the Philippines to be discharged from the U.S. Navy, at least two hundred thousand people participated in a peaceful march in Washington DC to demonstrate against racial prejudice in the United States. I felt so much pride and joy to see so many white people joining the march. And the "I have a dream" speech given by Dr. Martin Luther King Jr. still rings loudly in my memory. I remember listening to a speech given by Dr. Martin Luther King Jr. at a benefit show for the Southern Christian Leadership Conference (SCLC) in Philadelphia. That was the second time in my short life I was honored to shake the man's hand. Dr. King's statements condemning U.S. involvement in the Vietnam Conflict would also play a large role in the 1960s revolution.

Early in the decade, African American and white college students, impatient with the slow pace of legal change regarding civil rights, staged sit-ins, Freedom Rides, and protests marches to challenge segregation in the Southern states. Their efforts led to the federal government passing the Civil Rights Act of 1964, prohibiting racial discrimination in public facilities. The Voting Rights Act of 1965, guaranteeing voting rights, was a major milestone, defeating Southern racial profiling that denied voting rights for African American people. The "Bloody Sunday" events during a protest march by civil rights activists, black and white, across a bridge in Selma, Alabama, led to the passage of the Voting Rights Act in 1965.

The civil rights movement inspired other groups to press for equal rights. The women's movement fought for equal education and employment opportunities and a transformation of traditional views about a woman's place in American society. Mexican Americans fought for bilingual education programs in schools, unionization of farmworkers, improved employment opportunities, and increased political power. Native Americans pressed for control over their land and resources and the preservation of Native American cultures and tribal self-government.

In a far-reaching effort to reduce poverty, alleviate malnutrition, extend medical care, provide adequate housing, and enhance the employability of the poor, President Lyndon Johnson launched his Great Society Program in 1964.

Here are several other events that occurred in the 1950s and 1960s that seared my emotions and fed my interpretation that the United States of America was in the midst of a racial revolution:

* The Mississippi murders of three civil rights workers trying to enforce voting rights for African Americans.
* The bombing of a black Baptist church in Birmingham, Alabama, that killed four young girls attending Bible studies.
* A Virginia biracial couple—she was African American and he was white—who were banished from living in their home state because they married. They married in Washington DC. The couple changed history in 1967 when the United States Supreme Court upheld their lawsuit against the state of Virginia for the right to marry. The ruling struck down laws banning racially mixed marriages in seventeen states.
* The practice of blockbusting by white realtors. This was the scam of showing African Americans homes for sale in predominantly white communities. The realtors knew that white people would sell their homes cheaply once African

Americans started to move into the communities. The realtors would buy those homes and then sell them to African Americans at a much higher price.

* The advent of the African American afro hairstyle.
* The beginning of African Americans giving their newly born children African first names.
* The African American "Black power" chant and salute.
* The African American "Black is beautiful" chant and salute.
* American black Muslims began preaching a form of black nationalism.
* The birth of the hippie movement, which was a great advocate for brotherhood, sisterhood, and love among all races and cultures. Hippies preached racial understanding through poems, writings, rhetoric, and songs.
* The founding of Kwanzaa, a unique African American celebration with focus on traditional African values of family, community, responsibility, commerce, and self-improvement. Kwanzaa was created to reaffirm and restore African American roots in African culture.
* An African American congresswoman named Shirley Chisholm running for president of the United States.
* The anti–Vietnam War statements made by beloved singer, dancer, and actress Eartha Kitt at a white luncheon hosted by President Johnson's wife, Lady Bird Johnson.
* Race riots in large cities.
* The assassination of Robert Kennedy.
* Civil protests against the war in Vietnam.
* The protests by African Americans citing the majority number of African Americans being drafted and killed in the Vietnam War.

Two of the most painful memories for Annie's child that occurred during the civil rights revolution were the murders of Viola Liuzzo, a white woman, NAACP member, and civil rights activist, and Dr. Martin Luther King.

The 1960s would prove to be a heartfelt, emotionally entangling phenomenon for Annie's child. Some of the events were mollifying, and others were capricious. The Vietnam War, ghetto rioting, and the militant antiwar movement contributed to the chaos of that decade. I was worried because of the unknown. I worried about a revolution that might collapse the federal government. I decided to rejoin the military and serve in the Vietnam War.

4

The Effect of Racism

An African American friend living in my neighborhood who was a bit older than me became my mentor on the issues of civil rights and equal justice. We had long discussions on the subject every weekend. It did concern me that he was a bit of a militant. I have never felt that violence was the way to achieve equality; indeed, nonviolence said far more. As I watched the violence perpetrated against the Freedom Riders and the Freedom Marchers, I realized that television would issue the message to the nation that profound, unequal justice prevails in American society and laws. My mentor was more accommodating to violence in his thoughts. He was leaning toward actions preached by the Black Panther Party and Malcolm X. A lot of black militant organizations emerged during that period. And I could understand what brought them to their doctrines, but I knew that militant uprisings would not win. Only the majority could accomplish their goal in that manner. Black-sponsored groups like the National Association for the Advancement of Colored People (NAACP), the Student Nonviolent Coordinating Corps (SNCC), and Dr. King's Southern Christian Leadership Conference (SCLC) made more sense. Let the world see the violence perpetrated against the innocent. The actions of the federal government against the Little Rock Nine protests convinced me early on that nonviolence was a more effective weapon. While I disagreed with my mentor, I did appreciate the intellectual gain I received from listening to him. I was not sure if my disagreement with his philosophy would dissolve our friendship. Later, two separate events took their toll on our discussions: the John Birch Society meeting and the traffic stop melee.

5

The John Birch Society

One person who had a strong impact in my life, Dennis, and I became friends before he went away to a university and I enlisted in the military. Dennis and I settled and resided in the same community in the 1960s, becoming close friends again. One weekend, during our discussions of racial problems within the United States, Dennis mentioned the John Birch Society. I had heard of it before. He explained that the John Birch Society was an ultraconservative group that believed that black people had their place within American society but should have limited access to freedom. My mentor had some of their propaganda that reeked of racism. I found out much later in life that one or two of our future United States presidents were members of the John Birch Society. Dennis mentioned that the John Birch Society would be giving a presentation at the local movie theater the next weekend. I promised to attend the presentation with him. This was an opportunity for me to experience real-life controversy instead of watching it on television. But it probably would have been better if we had gone to the theater with picket signs.

The theater was a regular big screen establishment with a stage area in front of the screen. The audience was comprised of white people of various ages. Dennis and I were the only African Americans in the audience. We sat in the audience, and it wasn't long before Dennis started shouting profanity and ridiculing the speaker's words. As he indulged in his tirade, I couldn't help but think that we were really outnumbered. He leaned over and encouraged me to participate in his vocal venom, but he kept interrupting until two local police officers walked in. One of them bent over and spoke in a low voice. "If you don't calm down right now, I'm going to have to escort you outside. "

I shot Dennis a reproaching glance. "We're looking at big trouble if you don't shut up." But the speaker continued, and so did Dennis's tirade.

The police came back in, grabbed us both by the arms, and took us outside. Dennis had to be dragged out because he would not walk out. They held us in the police car without handcuffs. They explained they would hold us until the police sergeant arrived. To my shock, the police sergeant was an African American man. After speaking to his officers, he went inside the theater. Dennis and I were driven to the local police headquarters and charged with disturbing the peace. We were put into separate interrogation rooms. The police sergeant came in and spoke to me. He looked at me for a moment before he spoke. "You won't be charged with disturbing the peace because witnesses said that you had been docile while your friend caused the disturbance. But was your reason for going to the event to cause trouble?"

I shook my head. "No. I was just curious to learn the doctrines of the organization."

He seemed satisfied with my answer and told me I was free to go. He told me they would be holding Dennis for a few hours on a misdemeanor charge.

I was curious about the sergeant's position on the police force, and I asked about his career. He told me that his brother was a policeman working the Flower Hill beat where I had lived most of my life. He told me that the reason he was advanced to sergeant so quickly was because of the large amount of African Americans moving into the area. The racial climate proved the need for an authoritative African American position on the police force.

I told him that his position was representative of the changes in American society. He smiled. "You did the right thing in not being vocal at that John Birch Society event."

I was fortunate not to have a criminal record from that episode. Dennis was let out of jail later that night. We discussed the event two days later. Dennis was very disappointed that I did not demonstrate against the event as he had done. Even so, we continued to get together on weekends to discuss the racial climate in America.

6

The Traffic Stop Melee

A few weeks later, on a Saturday, Dennis and I left his house to get some snacks while we talked. My friend was driving. On the way down the road, a car full of rowdy white guys pulled up behind us. They were close on our tail, and we could hear them screaming and shouting at us to move faster. My friend became extremely angry. He called them "white assholes" and slapped the dashboard of the car just before we stopped at a red traffic light. As soon as we stopped, Dennis put the car in park and pulled up the hand brake. I asked what he was doing. He said, "Stay here."

I could hear him complaining loudly to the driver of the other car that he was driving too fast and too close. I turned to watch through the rear window. Dennis reached into the car and angrily slapped the driver in the face! The driver jumped out of the car, as did the other occupants of the vehicle. I got out of the car in an effort to break up the fight. There were five white guys and the two of us. We were surrounded. The driver of the car had pulled off his belt, which had a large buckle, and was cursing at Dennis, who was backing around in a circle to avoid being hit by the belt.

One of those guys came up behind me and held me in an armlock so I could not help Dennis. By this time, there was a line of traffic behind us that could not get through the intersection. One white lady, who had pulled up behind our cars, got out of her car and came toward us. She was shouting, "Stop this! Stop this! We all have to learn to live together as people!" She was in the middle of that circle.

At that moment, the fellow behind me let go of my arms. The white group got back in their car. Dennis and I got back into our car. The lady got back into her car, and we all went our separate ways.

Dennis let out a long sigh. "I was going to really get into it with the driver of the other car, had that lady not come along to break it up."

I asked, "Why did you slap the guy?"

He shrugged. "The driver said, 'Get out of my face, nigger.' That's why I slapped him. I really wanted to beat the hell out of that guy."

I told him, "Violence won't solve anything."

He stared at me for a moment before saying, "At least I'm not a coward. You acted like a coward during that fight by letting yourself get put in an armlock."

I glared at him. "I didn't get out of the car to fight. I got out of the car to stop the fighting."

"African Americans have to fight back to stop the whites from pushing us around."

I frowned. "That lady had shown us how we should act."

Dennis brushed away my opinion. "She was just being patronizing so she could get on down the road."

I disagreed with him, and he asked, "What makes you so sure?"

I stated, "The tears in her eyes when she was saying the words."

Dennis and I did not get together for discussions very often after that incident. I heard from another source that he thought of me as cowardly. That did not bother me, because I have inward strength against racism, and it did not require the use of violence.

7

The Viola Liuzzo Murder

Viola Liuzzo was born the same month and year as Mother Annie. The following article is an excellent biography about the Viola Liuzzo murder and can be found at the following Web site: http://law.jrank.org/pages/8327/Liuzzo-Viola-Fauver-Gregg. html.

Viola Fauver Gregg Liuzzo

Civil rights activist and martyr Viola Gregg Liuzzo was murdered after the 1965 voting rights march from Selma, Alabama, to Montgomery, Alabama. A thirty nine year old wife, mother and student, Liuzzo had spontaneously driven from her home in Detroit to help with the historic march. While transporting other participants back to Selma afterward, she was killed by members of the Ku Klux Klan (KKK). The tragedy both shocked and inspired U.S. citizens. President Lyndon B. Johnson decried her slaying on national television, and her death gave impetus for passing the landmark Voting Rights Act of 1965. Two Alabama juries failed to convict her assassins, who were ultimately found guilty of conspiracy. Nearly two decades later, her family brought an unsuccessful $2 million dollar lawsuit against the Federal Bureau of Investigation (FBI), following congressional revelations that the bureau may have known about but done nothing to stop Klan plans to kill the marchers. Liuzzo's memory is honored by memorials in Alabama and commemorations in Detroit.

Liuzzo was born in the coal-mining town of California, Pennsylvania, on April 11, 1925. She dropped out of school in the tenth grade and worked as a waitress. In 1950, she married Anthony James Liuzzo, a business agent of the International Brotherhood of Teamsters, with whom she had three children.

Liuzzo returned to school and, in 1962, she graduated with top honors from the Carnegie Institute of Detroit. She found employment as a medical library assistant. Though a high school dropout, she loved reading, and introduced her children to the works of philosopher Henry David Thoreau. She explained to them his theory of civil disobedience, a concept that would find widespread support during the civil rights movement.

Despite her lack of formal education, Liuzzo won acceptance to Wayne State University. By 1965, she was studying Shakespeare and philosophy. Like other students across the United States, she became increasingly concerned about violence against civil rights workers. The civil rights movement was at a crossroads: it had achieved important gains against segregation, but now it faced resistance and violence as it sought to win voting rights for African Americans living in the South.

In early March 1965, a pivotal event in civil rights history pushed the movement forward and changed Liuzzo's life. The murder of Jimmie Lee Jackson at the hands of Alabama troopers had motivated civil rights leaders to stage a protest march from Selma, Alabama, to the capitol in Montgomery, fifty miles away. The march would be lead by Martin Luther King Jr., president of the Southern Christian Leadership Conference (SCLC); Ralph J. Bunche, an African American Nobel laureate and diplomat to the United Nations; and other dignitaries. Once at the capitol, they planned to confront Governor George Wallace, an unbending foe of integration. But, as in previous civil rights protests, Wallace's state troopers struck first. On March 7, hundreds of African Americans set out from Selma, only to be stopped minutes later by club-wielding police officers and troopers. As law enforcement beat men, women, and children, millions of horrified U.S. citizens watched on television. Liuzzo and her family were among the viewers.

Within days, protests erupted nationwide. In Washington, D.C., some six hundred people picketed outside the White House. In Detroit, Liuzzo joined 250 students in a march on local FBI offices. Wherever protests occurred, people demanded federal protection for civil rights workers and the passage of new voting rights legislation. King announced a new march from Selma to Montgomery. Before it could begin on March 9, federal judge Frank M. Johnson, fearing new violence, postponed it. Two days later, another civil rights worker— the reverend James J. Reeb, a Unitarian minister from Boston—died at the hands of violent whites in Selma.

On March 15, President Lyndon B. Johnson appeared on television to address both houses of Congress. He called for passage of the voting rights bill and also gave his full support to the marchers in Selma. That night, Liuzzo attended a meeting at which several Wayne State students said they would join the march. She decided to go. She packed a few clothes in a shopping bag, and by the next afternoon was driving south.

Liuzzo was one of thousands arriving at the church that served as the launching point for the march, Brown Chapel. Appointed to the reception desk to help with last-minute chores, she greeted new arrivals. As was her way, she wanted to do more, and soon she had volunteered the use of her car for transporting others.

On March 21, the journey to Montgomery began as marchers passed a vast contingent of federal security. Governor Wallace had ruled out protecting the marchers as being too expensive, but President Johnson had made available military police, FBI agents, U.S. Marshals, and nineteen hundred members of the Alabama national guard who were placed under federal control. There was to be no repeat of the violence committed two weeks earlier by Alabama troopers.

The five-day march ended in a gathering of twenty-five thousand people at the capitol in Montgomery where King once again preached his doctrine of nonviolence. Yet he warned of further struggles ahead.

"IT'S EVERYBODY'S FIGHT. THERE ARE TOO MANY
PEOPLE WHO JUST STAND AROUND TALKING."
—VIOLA LIUZZO

Now that the march was over, Liuzzo prepared to make good on her promise of driving people back to Selma. Staff members of the SCLC advised her that further help was unnecessary, given the buses already waiting. Liuzzo nevertheless drove three women and a man to their destination and by nightfall, was returning to Selma again, this time with nineteen-year-old Leroy Moton, an African American barber and civil rights worker. In the swamplands of Lowndes County, a car chased them down and its occupants shot and killed Liuzzo. Moton, covered with Liuzzo's blood, feigned death and then ran three miles before finding safety with other civil rights workers.

It took the FBI eight hours to arrest three suspects, all Klan members. Gary Thomas Rower, Jr., a thirty-four-year-old Klan member who had been passing information to the FBI for years, was riding with the three others in the car from which the fatal shots were fired. Immediately, the state of Alabama indicted the other three men on first-degree murder charges. Rowe was given immunity and put in protective custody in return for testifying against Eugene Thomas, age forty-three; William Orville Eaton, age forty-one; and Collie Leroy Wilkens, Jr., age twenty-one. According to Rowe's subsequent testimony, the men had received instructions from Klan leaders to punish one of the marchers.

A trial on state charges in May 1965 ended in a mistrial. However, a subsequent federal trial, based on a conspiracy to violate Liuzzo's civil rights, brought guilty verdicts. Each of the defendants was sentenced to ten years. A subsequent appeal failed.

In 1979 the Liuzzo family filed a $2 million lawsuit against the FBI. The suit accused the bureau of negligence in its hiring, training, and supervision of Rowe. The informant, it alleged, was a loose gun who had actively participated in the murder. U.S. district judge Charles Joiner heard the trial without a jury and on May 30, 1983, found that Rowe did not shoot Liuzzo. He further ruled that the government was not responsible for her death.

In 1982, the Detroit City Council honored Liuzzo for her contributions to the struggle for civil and human rights. In June 1982, a mayoral proclamation made June 1-8 Viola Liuzzo Commemoration Week. Other memorials followed. In 1985, nearly one hundred marchers led by the Reverend Joseph Lowery, president of the SCLC, retraced the historic Selma-to-Montgomery march and laid a wreath at the site where she was murdered. There along U.S. Route 80, beside a swampy stretch, stands a simple stone marker, dedicated in 1991 by women members of the SCLC. It reads, "In Memory of Our Sister Viola Liuzzo Who Gave Her Life in the Struggle for the Right to Vote."

End of article.

8

The Martin Luther King Murder

Annie's child suffered through an immense emotional trauma after learning about the murder of Dr. Martin Luther King Jr. in April of 1968. Here was a man I had accepted as the great emancipator of African American people, and now he was dead. I went through the shock, the anger, the grief, and the acceptance that many Americans had to face. The anger, however, was not quietly endured by many, as shown by the riots that some African Americans perpetrated against the American establishment. The feelings that many African Americans displayed after this tragic event fed my fear that the nation was in the midst of a civil war. What bothered me most during the following days was my inability to look into the face of Caucasian people without feeling disdain. To my surprise, I learned later that many of my Caucasian neighbors felt the same disdain that a white person had committed this crime.

Later I attended an event that opened my pain to learning about human beings. A white pastor in our segregated community initiated a meeting with the pastor of the African American church to discuss racial unity. The heartfelt welcome for the pastor's predominately white congregation to attend our church was met with great enthusiasm. The sermons were great, and a sense of community prevailed. At the very next gathering, this time in the white church a week later, I witnessed the true spirit of the white community condemning racism and the so-called white supremacy ideology that most whites identified with the Southern states. The meetings continued, the discussions continued, and the community thrived, working together on the same level. The community that I lived in is still thriving today and is now an interracial community. Participating in that community process was at the time the nearest I had ever come to healing from the emotional scarring of living with overt and institutional discrimination.

Part Five

Vietnam

1

The Door to Death

In the year 1968, the electric company I was employed with decided to discontinue the small electric motor repair winding business. Small motor winding repair was becoming unprofitable. You could purchase a new motor at close to the same price as having one rewound. Before the layoffs came, the company offered me a job as an apprentice in their large motor winding division. That division plant, however, was many miles away, which made it a hardship for me to commute or live nearby.

I began to think about going back to construction work again. One day, weeks later, as I was returning from a construction interview and walking down Broad Street in Philadelphia, I noticed a U.S. Navy recruiting office. The thought of reenlisting went through my mind. "They won't take me," I thought. "I'm twenty-seven. I'm too old." I walked to the door anyway.

"Hey, come in," said a recruiter. The recruiter not only said I could come back to the Seabees, but he also promised I could start out with an E-4 rank and no boot camp. He said that because of the Vietnam War it was easy for former servicemen to get back into the military. And he stated that most of the Seabee battalions were deploying to Vietnam. I was not that happy about going to a war zone, but I did miss the construction trades and unit goals associated with being in a battalion. I missed the synergy of construction and solving problems as a team. It is a fast and different pace compared to civilian construction techniques.

So I reenlisted. I flew to Port Hueneme, California, to join Naval Mobile Construction Battalion Four (NMCB-4). Returning to the U.S. Navy after five years, I noticed that African Americans were more visible, even among commissioned officers and higher enlisted ranks. Nevertheless, I didn't sense any significant change by white military members in their overall attitudes about African Americans.

After attending utilities man boiler engineering school for three months, I deployed to Vietnam in May 1969, while the Vietnam War was at its peak. The moment I stepped off the plane in Da Nang, Vietnam, I was shocked by the environment. At the airport, everyone was wearing a sidearm or walking around with an assault rifle. Around the outside of the airport, I could hear the sounds of bombings and sirens sounding off, indicating attacks from the enemy. I thought to myself, "Oh boy, Annie's child is in big trouble now."

Being back with the construction Seabees was greatly satisfying. Seabees accomplished astounding feats in Vietnam, as they had done in World War II. In addition to the military infrastructure, Seabee teams built and repaired schools, dug water wells, provided medical supplies and treatment, built living quarters, and provided food for the many needy civilians in war-torn villages. The Seabee can-do spirit would become part of an individual member's mind-set once the construction work began. The Seabee teams in Vietnam proved to be a family with the civilian populace.

Sadly though, racial disharmony between African Americans and whites still existed within the military units in Vietnam. I was the "water king" in Camp Adenir, a thirty-two-acre Seabee base next to the Da Nang U.S. Naval Hospital, a stone's throw from the Da Nang River. The water king is the person who supplies, treats, and monitors the distribution of potable water to the military campsite facilities.

My crew of Seabees processed, purified, and pumped all the water and steam for the base camp's galley, mess hall, laundry, and living quarters. I had made E-5 rank by this time and had seven subordinates in my charge. At any given time, approximately three of the guys, including myself, were African Americans.

Racial tension in the ranks of the American foot soldiers, which often broke into violence, was common during the Vietnam Conflict. Anyone who wasn't there would be amazed at the extent of racial strife that threatened military discipline and integrity. The belief that black soldiers were being killed in disproportionate numbers plus the many racial incidents within the military brought the African American soldier to his lowest morale since the exclusionary rules of World War II. The racial strife within the Vietnam military was a reflection of the racial disharmony in the United States. Our Seabee units consisted of white people from the Deep South, urban African Americans from the Northern states, and everywhere in between. Trying to get black and white people to get along while living and working together was tough. Certain people would routinely call others nigger, peckerwood, or similar derogatory remarks. One African American Seabee aimed his assault weapon on a white cook in the galley and had to be persuaded not to pull the trigger. One ensign commissioned officer in our camp, renowned for being a bigot, was the victim of a grenade-fragging incident; a fragmentation grenade was thrown into his living quarters one night. He survived with only slight wounds but lost his confrontational racist attitude after that incident.

It was during my tour of duty in Vietnam, where death was a daily reality, that I gained a belief that Annie's child had reached the end of life's road. But I was one of the fortunate ones. Our commanding officer at the time designated me the unit representative for hearing racial disharmony complaints and relaying those complaints to him for resolution. Whenever issues would arise, I would sit down with the parties involved and try to rectify the problem. I actually held racial sensitivity sessions for our Seabee unit in Vietnam. I learned a lot about people while I was in that position, especially how people's feelings and perceptions affect their behavior. That experience in Vietnam allowed me to have a positive contribution to race relations within the U.S. military.

2

Change in the U.S. Navy

I was privileged to be a part of historic changes that transformed the U.S. Navy into a more just fighting force. By the early 1970s, the Seabee demographic was changing. More African Americans were being accepted into the construction ratings than ever before, and for me the changes paid dividends in advancement and duty assignments.

Evolving from the racial turmoil in Vietnam was the thinking of a Navy admiral, the late Elmo Zumwalt Jr., whose willingness to embrace change had an enormous effect on race relations in the Navy. Admiral Zumwalt was appointed as chief of naval operations (CNO) in 1970. One of Admiral Zumwalt's goals was to encourage personnel recruitment and retention by making Navy service more desirable for all sailors. Admiral Zumwalt communicated with naval personnel via his famous Z grams, which were circulated to every Navy base, station, and ship in every corner of the world. Z grams were used to announce regulatory and disciplinary policies. The Z gram that affected me the most was Z gram 66: "Equal Opportunity in the Navy." Z-66 and subsequent steps taken by Admiral Zumwalt took on the huge challenge of erasing institutional racism and blatant operational prejudices in the Navy. Z-66 addressed a number of irritants that made Navy life difficult for African Americans. For instance, at that time, it was hard for African Americans to find barbers who knew how to cut African American hair. With Z-66, every base and station was required to employ people who were experienced in cutting African American hair. In addition, African Americans could not readily obtain grooming aids, hair care products, reading materials, such as *Ebony* and *Jet* magazines, and many other products culturally oriented toward African Americans in the base stores and commissaries. Thanks to Z-66, all stations had to carry these products. Some might have called these changes cosmetic, but they meant a lot to those of us who were affected.

Even more important was Z-66's mandate for every base, station, and ship to have a minority affairs assistant with direct access to the commanding officer. This position was the predecessor of the Equal Opportunity Advisor program, which assigned upward communication responsibilities as a collateral duty to officers and senior enlisted persons. All personnel, not just commanding officers, had access to the Z grams. As a result, everybody knew what the CNO was ordering. There was no hiding the new policies. Admiral Zumwalt was a wise man. He listened, observed what was happening, knew resistance would arise—even among those with good intentions—and pushed through the changes. Admiral Zumwalt became greatly admired by naval personnel and their dependents for his change efforts. He even secured the affectionate nickname Uncle Zumwalt.

3

Music

During the 1950s and 1960s, country and western music was considered a symbol of racism by the majority of African American military servicemen. The Southern hillbilly slang seemed to represent the Ku Klux Klan–type racist attitudes of the Southern areas. During my deployment to Vietnam, I became close friends with a fellow Seabee, who happened to be white, whose family was living at our battalion home port, Port Hueneme, California. After the battalion returned to home port from Vietnam, I spent a lot of time with Ken, his wife, Joy, two daughters, and a son. I really appreciated being accepted as part of the family. Ken was originally from Florida and Joy from Oregon. My racial makeup was never an issue in our friendship.

I was living in the barracks at the home port but usually visited "my family"—at their behest—each night for dinner. I really enjoyed being with their young children, who enjoyed being with me, especially when we went out to the malls or an amusement park. I spent many a night babysitting the kids while Ken and Joy went out to the movies or elsewhere. It was truly like having my own family there. Ken and Joy enjoyed country and western music, which I learned to enjoy in their home. Ken and Joy invited me to go to a local country and western club one night. They hired a teenage neighbor who was also a good friend of the family as a babysitter.

As we were entering the nightclub, a bouncer at the door reached out and put a hand on my chest. The bouncer asked what I was doing there, and before I could answer, Joy said in a bit of anger, "He's with us. Why are you questioning him?" Joy was clearly agitated by the bouncer's actions, and the bouncer made a quick apology to me. When we got inside, I could feel the unwelcoming environment immediately. The musicians playing on stage and the people dancing began to stare at us. I did realize, a few minutes later, that I was the only African American in the place.

The three of us sat at an empty table and began talking. Joy was getting upset again because the waitresses kept walking by our table. Joy got up after ten minutes and asked one of the waitresses to come to our table. In the meantime, Ken and I started to comment about the way people were staring at our table. Later, as the three of us were sitting there talking, eating, and drinking beer, Joy was frustrated by people staring at our table. I appreciated that they did not realize what was happening until I explained the situation. I explained that I was the only African American there, and that was the reason people were staring. I explained further about the stigma of racism in country and western music. Ken and Joy were genuinely surprised. Joy then made the comment that if the people staring were racist, then, "That's their problem, not ours."

As the night went on, I started enjoying the music and watching Ken and Joy dancing together. The staring diminished, and the waitresses were tending our table as expected. And later, some of the guys from our battalion walked in with their wives and girlfriends and sat at a table next to ours. The guys expressed surprise that I was there. One guy stated that most African American guys he knew did not like country and western music. I stated that I had grown to like it from Ken and Joy. So we continued to talk, joke, and listen to music. After awhile, when Ken got up to go to the restroom, a slow song was playing and Joy prodded me into dancing with her, at the cheers of the other guys.

As Joy and I swayed to the sound of the music, I was surprised at how easy it was to blend rhythm and blues and rock and roll dancing with the sound of country music. As Joy and I danced to the music, someone tore my arm away from Joy's waist, and this guy, obviously drunk, said, "We don't allow niggers dancing with white girls here."

To my surprise and before I could react, Joy slapped him and hollered, "Don't you call him that!"

Ken had just returned from the restroom and saw what was happening. Ken grabbed the guy and spun him to the floor. Then two of the military guys at the table next to us grabbed the drunk and dragged him toward the entry door. Friends of the drunk then got into the melee. A huge brawl ensued. Ken, Joy, and I went back to our table. The bouncer broke up the fight. I felt terrible, as if the whole incident was my fault. The drunk and his friends were told to leave the club. The military guys were also told to leave. The bouncer came to our table and informed us that he had called the local police and the military police. The bouncer then asked that we stay at the table until the police arrived. The band kept playing. Ken kept insisting that Joy and I go dance again, but I felt too bad. I felt ashamed that I had caused this problem.

After the police arrived, they determined that the incident had not been caused by our military friends or us. The police escorted the drunk and his friends away from the club and advised us to leave also. On the drive home, I really felt the closeness of Ken, Joy, and myself. Joy was driving with Ken in the front seat, me in the backseat. There was complete silence for a few miles. Then Ken noticed that Joy was driving away from home and toward the beach. When Ken asked her why she was driving that way, she said, "We need to talk."

When we got to the beach parking area, Joy asked me to stay at the car while she and Ken took a walk along the beach. I was mystified. So was Ken. We looked at each other, wondering what was going on. As they walked along the beach, I kept feeling bad about ruining the evening. After about thirty minutes, Ken waved to me to join them at the water's edge. As we sat there, what Joy said to me was astounding—not only because of her physical appearance but also because she had hidden a portion of her life from her husband, which she had told him about in the thirty minutes they walked along the beach.

Joy was born in Alabama to black parents. Her mother was half white, due to a rape from a white owner of the sharecropper farms common at the time. Due to the racism attitudes that existed at the time and the fact that she looked completely white, they gave her up for adoption when she was three years old at the advice of local "black officials." She was put into a local white orphanage and three years later was adopted by a military couple stationed in a nearby state. The couple settled in Oregon. Joy did not find out about her adoption until years later when she was a teenager. Her parents convinced her that revealing that she had African American blood would be detrimental for her whole life. After seeing and hearing the racism that existed in America, she agreed and buried her true identity within herself. Joy and Ken met and married years later when he was stationed in Oregon.

As I heard her story, I kept wondering how Ken was feeling, but I did not ask. He seemed okay with what she was saying. She stated that she was extremely worried that their kids might display some African American physical features, but they did not, to her relief. I looked at Ken for a moment, still wondering how he was feeling, and he looked at me and said, "Believe me, this is not a problem with me."

We were all silent on the drive back home. I could not help but think what a shame it was that we lived in a society where people had to hide their bloodline from other people. After we got home and after the babysitter left, Joy asked me to stay the night, and I said yes, even though my barracks sleeping area was only fifteen minutes away from the military family housing area. After two hours of sleeping, I awakened to the sound of Ken and Joy talking in the next room. Ken told Joy that he too had grown up with a racist attitude. He said that his parents instilled in him that attitude in various ways and that his father once said that black people were "African animals." Joy stated that she never realized Ken's parents were racist because his parents had never shown that type of attitude when she was in their presence. Ken stated that his own attitude had changed when he was serving his first military tour in Vietnam. A black military co-worker had literally saved his life one day during an attempted base siege by the Vietcong. Ken and I had spoken once about that action, but I never knew about this life-saving event.

He then stated that he relayed his changed attitude about black people to his parents during a visit after that Vietnam tour. Ken then stated to Joy that the reason Joy did not know about his parent's racist feelings was because he had relayed Joy's feelings to his parents long before he and Joy married. Ken then stated that out of respect for both of their feelings, his parents would never reveal their racist attitudes while the two of them were in their presence.

Listening to that conversation made me feel a lot better. I began to feel that the whole horrible night was worth it because of the communication it sparked between a husband and wife. I could not, however, forget the pain of that stabbing word from that drunk—nigger. The emotional pain of hearing that word is hard to explain. But Annie's child had to move on.

4

Moving On

From Vietnam, NMCB-4 deployed to Okinawa as a ready battalion, to be assigned for quick forward deployment as needed, in support of any conflict, military warfare, or peacetime emergency. The Okinawa military racial climate had changed significantly for the better since my first deployment there back in the early 1960s. The Japanese subservient behavior toward Americans was gone. In addition, the U.S. government had adopted plans to return sovereignty of the Okinawa and Ryukyu island chain back to Japan.

After our deployment from Okinawa in 1971, I was reassigned to U.S. Naval Station Kodiak, Alaska, where for first time I met an African American civil engineering commissioned officer. He was assigned to the Public Works Center, one of the commanding officer's staff. In addition, we had a female Seabee working in our division; she was part of a pilot program to enlist females into the construction rating. Also existing was a program for commissioning females into the Civil Engineer Corps. Furthermore, the Warrant Officer Program was also touted as a way for Seabee-enlisted minorities, including females, to earn a commission in the Civil Engineer Corps. I became aware that the policy changes mandated by the Z grams were very real. I was witnessing steady progress.

Subsequently I was assigned to NMCB-3, also home ported at Port Hueneme, California. We deployed to Okinawa, where I became part of a detachment to Taiwan, Republic of China. As a member of NMCB-3, I observed enormous changes in the racial demographic of Seabee units. Minority staffing had improved tremendously in a short time. Although cultural clashes and tension still occurred, tools to deal with these problems were in place, thanks to Admiral Zumwalt's policies. I was assigned collateral duty as an equal opportunity advisor for the battalion, serving on the commanding officer's staff. This duty afforded me an opportunity for specialized training in the field of race relations. Continuous race relations education for staff and field troops was a key factor in fostering a harmonious racial environment. I felt a part of historic change.

My next duty assignment was with Reserve Construction Battalion 13 (RNMCB-13) located at Naval Air Station Brooklyn, New York, in 1973. I was assigned there as the sole active duty person to help manage the reservist training in maintenance and operations of all construction equipment assigned to the battalion. I recall walking into that headquarters office and being greeted by an African American officer with four stripes—a captain in the Navy Civil Engineer Corps! It was a shock, but a welcome one, and it was a pleasure for me to serve on his staff.

This assignment was very different, in that I was working with people who were part-time military. These Seabee reservists, who generally worked as military people one weekend a month, brought along with them the racial tensions and conflicts endemic to a large, racially polarized city. While I was stationed there, I was constantly reminded of how the U.S. military active duty forces had become a far more racially harmonious entity than the civilian community. Even the corporate and political worlds could not equal the progress of the U.S. military at the time.

My next assignment took me to U.S. Naval Station Holy Loch, Scotland. There I was fortunate enough to be promoted to chief petty officer, working in the Public Works Center. The Seabee contingent there numbered a few dozen individuals, and I found myself the only African American assigned there at the time. The Scotland assignment was especially enjoyable because I lived in off-base housing, socialized with locals, and was blessed with the opportunity to trace my genealogical roots back to the Scotch–Irish part of my bloodline, derived from my maternal grandfather.

After two years in Scotland, I was assigned to Public Works Center, Naval Station Guantanamo Bay, Cuba. A uniquely different duty station, Guantanamo is a sprawling chunk of tropical paradise under U.S. military control grafted onto a corner of a Communist country. My duties there included a senior leadership position within a division of the Public Works Center as well as a collateral position as the naval station equal opportunity advisor (EOA). The Seabee population at Guantanamo was large, and for the first time in my Navy career, I confidently felt that the minority and female components of the Seabees were closely reflective of American society.

In my EOA duties at Guantanamo, I dealt with complaints about promotions not granted, racial discrimination charges, racist dialogue between sailors, friction between civilian Jamaican employees and military people, and many other issues. I facilitated human relations sensitivity training on a regular basis, helping people of different races and cultures understand each other. Thanks in part to these sensitivity classes, the Seabee community at Guantanamo took the lead in racial harmony, measured by the lowered number of racially motivated incidents and discrimination complaints during my eighteen-month assignment there.

Even so, there were many difficult issues to overcome in my EOA collateral duty assignment. I recall one case in which a division master chief petty officer approved an African American's positive evaluation but denied him a promotion, not just once, but twice. The sailor's service record was equal to or better than others who were promoted.

The case came to me, and I concluded the discrimination complaint was justified. The master chief was telling the commanding officer that I was wrong in my assertion. I encountered my own peer pressure within the chief's community because I was going against the word of a master chief. But I had a job to do. As command equal opportunity advisor, I didn't have to report only to my commanding officer but could go over his head to the Chief of Naval Personnel Office in Washington DC. After my commanding officer denied my assertion of discrimination against the sailor, I told my commanding officer that I would have to resolve the issue through the Chief of Naval Personnel's Office. I did that and eventually received word that the complaint was ruled in favor of the complainer. It was a risk, but when I left Guantanamo, the commanding officer wrote me a very positive evaluation, and that was one of the factors that helped me get promoted to the rank of senior chief petty officer.

Guantanamo Bay was the most satisfying assignment in my naval career in that I was making a difference in improving race relations within the U.S. Navy. Perhaps in part because of the positive racial climate, Guantanamo Bay, Cuba, became one of the most requested duty stations in the Navy.

My next assignment was the most educational about minority civilian perception of the military. After several interviews, I was accepted for my next assignment as a manpower detailer—the person who matches Seabee sailors with their duty assignments. I was in charge of the assignment of Seabees in the construction utilities and construction electrician ratings throughout the Navy. I arrived in the Washington DC area to work this assignment in May 1980. My four-year stay as a detailer allowed for conversations with thousands of Seabees and frequent travel to Seabee duty stations around the world.

We were called detailers. Detailers are very instrumental in retaining people in the Navy by helping them obtain the duty stations they prefer. It was not long before I discovered that far too many African American Seabees did not want to reenlist, no matter where I promised to assign them. Far too many African American Seabees were telling me, "I don't want to reenlist because I don't think I can make higher rank, and I can do far better in civilian life." One-third of my Seabee assignment charges were African American. What an astounding success statistic that was over just two decades! But I was losing far too many on secondary recruitment!

After all the racial demographic progress I had witnessed during my tours of duty, it seemed the progress had stalled. I couldn't help but wonder what was going on. When I investigated the situation, I learned that low minority recruiting and reenlistment was a problem Navy-wide, and nothing seemed to be in effect to change the situation. Ironically, the belief among many African Americans at the time—that they had little chance of promotion in the Navy—was not based on reality. One big problem was the African American civilian perception. I knew this perception would not be easy to overcome. After my assignment as a Seabee detailer was completed, I decided to take on the challenge of African American Seabee recruitment. A number of programs came about in the early 1980s to address minority recruitment and retention. The Senior Minority Recruiting Program (SMRP) sent senior minority personnel to join general recruiting tours around the country. The senior minority presence was intended to show minority students in high schools that they too could advance to senior leadership positions in the Navy.

After my assignment as detailer was completed, I volunteered for interim duty with the SMRP program. Traveling with a recruiting team throughout New York State—from New York City to Buffalo—I learned much about this new generation and their thoughts about the military. There was a lot of negativity to overcome. The American divisiveness about the Vietnam War was a contributor to the skepticism of young people, especially minorities, because of the disproportionate number of African Americans who were killed during the Vietnam War. To my astonishment, I had high school students ask me, "If the United States gets into another war, are they going to send just black people out to fight the war?" They were serious. They did not know how ridiculous that question sounded to me as a soldier who had experienced the Vietnam War and saw the deaths of many men, both black and white.

Many of the minority high school students did pay a little more attention when they met me, a senior enlisted person who was African American. Some would see my E-8 uniform stripes and ask me, "Isn't E-9 the highest rank you can make as an enlisted person in the military?" I felt proud to answer and told them that if I could do it, they could do the same.

Other barriers for minority student were gang influence and peer pressure. Some students would shy away from our recruiting sessions, and later approach me privately because they did not want their friends seeing they were interested. Some would ask me, if they went to a recruiter, could the recruiter keep it a secret? They wanted to walk away from the neighborhood but were not sure they had the power to leave. When I thought about the environment some of these students faced, I became passionate about what the military could offer them. I like to believe I helped a few of those students make the decision to join the renowned ranks of the Navy Seabees.

After completing a final tour of duty in Japan, I transferred to fleet reserve retirement in 1987 and settled in Honolulu, Hawaii. Looking back, the minority and female demographic in the military in general had come a long way, and years later, from what I understand from veteran Seabee acquaintances, the Seabees now have an excellent African American representation and a positive trend in minority affairs.

PART SIX
Hawaii

1

Hawaii: The People

Hawaii is a treasure of racial diversity. Hawaii is the true racial melting pot that Dr. King alluded to in some of his speeches. This year marks the forty-first anniversary of the murder of Dr. Martin Luther King Jr. Annie's child is living in the island state of Hawaii, which celebrates the birth of Dr. King each year with a parade sponsored by various groups of all races and cultures, along a famous Waikiki tourist route. It was a long journey to get back to Hawaii. I felt the need to live there as far back as my first travel to the new state in 1960, on my way to Midway Island. In Hawaii I feel the comfort of racial diversity.

After retiring from the military in February 1987, I decided that I really needed to live in Hawaii. Relieving the pain of American racism was easier in Hawaii for a number of reasons—the most outstanding circumstance was the absence of the Caucasian majority. The trauma of the racial strife from childhood to my age when I moved to Hawaii, forty-five, turned full circle. Today, I truly feel like I am home.

Hawaii is a beautiful and unique state—the Aloha State. *Aloha* is a native Hawaiian word that symbolizes the friendship and togetherness of its residents. The hugs or the "shaka" sign given upon seeing a friend or being introduced to a stranger is a tradition in Hawaii that exemplifies the loving nature of Hawaiian residents. There is an old saying, "When in Rome, do as the Romans do." In Hawaii, this is done with little effort. Hawaii is a state where the "minority majority" exists. We have many different ancestries here, including Native Hawaiians, Pacific Islanders, Japanese, Chinese, Koreans, Southeast Asians, Filipinos, Caucasians, African Americans, Europeans, Hispanics, Portuguese, Spanish, and Australians. There exists in Hawaii a beautifully unified mix of racial diversity. There is no polarization of races in Hawaii.

Hawaii is not like living "on base" in another country. Here in Hawaii, we don't just exist as people together, we live as people together. Hawaii's residents have an intercultural bond unlike any other place in the United States. By virtue of a limited land mass, we are bonded to each other. We enjoy each other's cultural differences to the point of intermingling those differences. Some of Hawaii's cultural heritage can be enjoyed in language, food, dance, clothing, education, travel, religion, history, and a host of other adventures. In Hawaii, interracial marriages are very common, including African American and Caucasian marriages, dubbed salt and pepper marriages in the popular vernacular.

2

Hawaii and Racial Disharmony

Like any other society, Hawaii's people do experience some disharmony. Racial hatred is not a norm in Hawaii but is carried inwardly in some people, perhaps through fear of being exposed to a society that is overwhelmingly accepting of race. Even though there is racial or cultural dislike by some people, tolerance is the norm. After settling in Hawaii, I learned that Caucasian people in Hawaii hear, see, and feel a lot of racial prejudice, which was just the reverse of my experience in America. The Hawaiian word *haole,* pronounced "howlie," is sometimes used to describe white people like the word *nigger* is used against African American people. The word *haole* actually refers to white-skinned foreigners in the Native Hawaiian language. In my journey in Hawaii, most communications of racial prejudice that I have seen are relatively mild in comparison to the history of racism on the mainland.

An insight into the gravity of racism in Hawaii might come from a major portion of the following newspaper article by a Latino gentleman named Pablo Wegesend. Mr. Wegesend's article was published in the Honolulu *Star-Bulletin* newspaper.

Race in Hawaii
Ignorance about Latinos pervades isles

Last year, bounty hunter Dog Chapman was recorded using the "N" word. He later claimed that he didn't know the "N" word was offensive to African Americans.

Last month, city councilman Rod Tam used the word "wetback" at a council meeting, in reference to illegal aliens. Tam claimed he didn't know that the word "wetback" was considered offensive to Mexican Americans.

The word "wetback" was originally used to mock Mexican immigrants who swam across the Rio Grande into the United States. However, the word is commonly used by anti-Mexican racists to insult and threaten anyone of Mexican ancestry, even those whose parents and grandparents were born in the United States. It is similar to the history of the word "haole," which was originally used to refer to "foreigners."

It doesn't look good for Hawaii, a state that likes to call itself "a paradise of racial tolerance," to have two prominent individuals display such ignorance on racial issues, especially when it comes to ethnic groups that don't have as many members here.

The fame of Barack Obama, the Democratic Presidential nominee, has exposed the isolation some African Americans feel in Hawaii. While Obama wasn't exposed to the level of hate here that was prominent in places like Alabama or Mississippi, he felt stereotyped or misunderstood growing up here.

End of article quotation.

Generations of people who live in Hawaii still use the word *colored* to describe an African American person. I recall that after an employment interview a few years ago, the locally born and raised secretary of the manager who had hired me later revealed to me that she was shocked that the manager, a Caucasian lady from the state of Georgia, had hired me because I am "colored" and all Southern people don't like "colored" people. When I stated to the secretary that not all Southern people felt that way, it was a learning experience for her.

The descriptive terms used in Hawaii to describe a race of people would shock most people who live on the mainland. It is considered the norm in Hawaii for local people to use race as an identity descriptor. The word *colored*, used to describe an African American, was passed down through the local generations that were not exposed to the post–World War II communications process. Even during that time, the late 1940s and 1950s, the word *Negro*, used to describe my race generally on the mainland, was not embedded in the minds of Hawaii locals.

3

The N Word

When I grew up in Chester, Pennsylvania, I was aware of the words *colored* and *Negro*. I have always felt a disgust at the use of both of those words to describe me. Even though the word *Negro*—a derivative of the word *Negroid*, a scientific racial category—is valid, I still feel uncomfortable at the use of both those words to describe me and others. My knowledge of my race mixture is only one factor that has prevented me from accepting these descriptions. The word *black* has also caused me concern. Although the word *black* is commonly used these days to describe a race of people, when I hear it, I feel a slight pin prick internally. The description, as I remember, was accentuated during the African American civil rights revolution. At the time "Black power" was the rally call. But I felt, even far before that time, that the description "black" was not appropriate.

My feelings were confirmed after I read and watched the Alex Haley historical television documentary *Roots* in 1974. My own family history of racial bloodline is similar to many African American bloodlines. A vast amount of Caucasian blood was mixed with black-skinned Africans during slavery, due to forced servitude. The babies born from these unions passed along the bloodline lineage. The results have been African American people of many different skin colors and shades, including the "black" shade. And so to me, the bloodline lineage dictates that "African American" is the more accurate description.

Growing up, I used the word *black* because it was the atmospheric norm. Inwardly, I completely abhorred the words *black* or *white* as descriptive terms. To me, the shade or color of a person's skin is an inaccurate generalization for any race. There are some people in America who look Caucasian yet carry a lineage of African American blood and vice versa. In addition, the word *black* in the American lexicon encompasses a lot of negative meanings that can get stuck in the psychology of the general public. Such terms as *blacklist, black mark, blackout,* and *blackmail* are examples. Even the word *darkness* is used to describe a bad period during life. I personally feel that in the subconscious minds of most Americans, of all races, the description of *black,* except for the accumulation of money or material things, represents evil. Conversely, the word *white* is used mostly in a positive manner, creating an opposite view in the mind.

I became aware of my feelings about racial descriptions during my conversations with Jane, the young girl from Poland, during high school. She asked, "Why are your people sometimes called black [a term offensive to African Americans at the time] when all are not black?" I immediately gave deference to my roots and thought about the illogical reference of this offensive term. I told her it was because most of the Negro people in America were descendants of Africans brought to the United States during slavery, and most white people at that time could only see us as black in color. She then stated that her relatives explained to her that she was now considered "Polish American" and asked me why we were not "African American."

I remember the 1950s, when most African Americans believed that white people thought of them as unintelligent and beneath them. The infamous *Amos 'n' Andy* show on television and prior Hollywood images of African Americans reinforced the idea. I can remember reading, some years later, about a psychological study of African American girls of that era that revealed that the girls preferred to have white dolls rather than black dolls. This phenomenon was blamed on the young girls' impressions of how the American Caucasian society viewed African American people. Many African American people at that time also tried to look white by chemically straightening their hair and by using creams to lighten their skin color. My father also used the hair-straightening formula. My Mother Annie can remember me as a young baby crawling around on the floor and burning my tongue by licking the hair formula Konk O Lina that had spilled on the floor. A doctor had to actually clip the end of my tongue for survival.

Another difference is that at the time, the word *nigger* was very offensive to African Americans. To even say the word was considered offensive. The word *nigger* was seldom used in African American lexicons. So it's easy to see why I am in total disagreement with African Americans who use the word in a self-descriptive manner or toward each other. The price paid by the many generations from African slaves, who were dubbed "niggers," should demand abhorrence from each of us. I have heard racially derogatory slurs too much in my lifetime. Such words as *kike, chink, slope head, nigger, flip, wetback, Jap, white trash,* and *spik* are but a few. I think these names and the attitudes for saying them perpetuate a sense of intolerable differences. If as a species we want to survive, we have to quit putting our energy into belittling each other and work together to solve other real problems.

PART SEVEN
The Doctrine of Change

1

Change in the United States

Change has affected all generations of the American people. This is why America's Founding Fathers included that the Constitution of the United States be subject to change, through amendments, at the behest of the majority of American people. A constitution is a broad statement of a society's expectations from its governing bodies. It sets out principles, not day-to-day rules and regulations. Legislative bodies handle the passages, and courts decide if they have done their job properly. Our Constitution sets out our inherent bill of rights, the basic structure of our government, the power to tax and spend, the power of government and states, elections, and broad social issues such as civil rights, privacy, and a template for our civil and criminal statutes.

I was recently reminded of how great the American Constitution's principles have helped change America when I attended a graduation ceremony for Honolulu Punahou High School. Nolan Ying Black—the son of the late John Black, my mentor and best friend later in life—graduated with honors. Nolan is the product of a Caucasian man and a Chinese woman and is fluent in the Chinese language Mandarin. Nolan is now attending a prestigious university on the U.S. mainland.

The diversity of the graduating class and of the audience was instantly obvious. When I graduated from high school, there was little racial mixing during the graduation ceremony. African Americans sat on one side, and Caucasians sat on the other side. One of the principal speakers at the graduation ceremony reminded the audience that U.S. presidential nominee Barack Obama graduated from Punahou High School in 1979. My thoughts after hearing this reminder took me back through the history of America. I thought of the great change coming from the Civil War and the vital civil rights bills that were passed in accordance with the principles of the U.S. Constitution, which now allowed for the first time in U.S. history a multiracial person with African blood the possibility of becoming president of the United States. How ironic that our multiracial presidential nominee really represented the minority majority of the whole world, because two-thirds of the world's population are people of color.

The emotional pain I suffered as a teenager watching the Little Rock Nine, who dared integrate the Little Rock, Arkansas, Central High School, in 1957, became a sense of pride after attending this graduation ceremony. Annie's child sends a great thank you to the Little Rock Nine! Thank you for your bravery, commitment, and fortitude! And a thank you to the brave parents of these young people, who dared to risk the lives of their loved ones for change! The equal justice sentiment caused by the Little Rock Nine integration victory caused a forthcoming racial and civil rights revolution in America.

Since I graduated high school in 1959, there has been a major change in African American and other minority positions within America. Prestigious minority positions over the years have included state governors, chief executive officers of major companies, senators, congressional representatives, Supreme Court justices, ambassadors to the United Nations, secretaries of state, astronauts, members of major educational institutions, and mayors of large cities, to name a few. These major changes have eased a lot of inward pain felt by my generation.

Now, in the year 2008, I am proud to witness a major political revolution. It is a presidential election year with the possibility of a man with African blood becoming the president of the United States of America!

PART EIGHT
Journalistic Review

1

Dan Rather

From the worldview article in Honolulu's *Midweek* magazine, June 11, 2008: "Overcoming a History of Racism."

> Those of us who write about politics have been calling this presidential race "historic" for long months now. The word historic became almost a reflective appendage and, like all things that become automatic, it became easy to stop thinking about its full implications.
>
> And then the primary election season ended, with a forceful reminder of just what it looks like when history is made.
>
> Your reporter grew up in Houston at a time when segregation was a basic fact of life. In adult life, one of your reporter's earliest assignments was covering Dr. Martin Luther King Jr., and the drive for black civil rights in the south of the 1960's. It's difficult to convey, to those who were not alive or of memory age during that era, just how different that time was and just how fierce the battles were. One did not have to search for racism in coded speech or subtle policy shadings....racism was an overt, brutal fact. Those who stood up for access to the most basic of American rights, including the right to vote, faced vile insults, savage beatings and even murder.
>
> This week, not much more than four decades after President Lyndon Johnson signed the voting rights act, Americans could turn on their television sets and see an African American accepting the mantle of his party. Regardless of what one might think of Barack Obama,

the candidate, or his policies, this is a remarkable measure of social distance traveled from our relatively recent national past. As a democratic super delegate from New Jersey, himself an African American, said this week, "in a million years I never thought I'd see this".

Exit polling from certain primary states, in which a significant and troubling percentage of voters was willing to tell pollsters that they would not cast a ballot for a black man, confirms what we may have suspected: we have not reached Dr. King's promised land. There are still plenty of Americans....Not all of whom consider themselves bigots....who judge a man by the color of his skin rather than the content of his character.

Our cultural and national history of racism is long, and overcoming this history will be the work of more than just a generation or two.

End of article quotation.

For Annie's child, in celebrating the election of the first African American president of the United States, it brings an emotional healing, to the emotional suffering I felt, on the journey through racism. Residing in the State of Hawaii, where the new president has ties, is the epitome of my healing process. The racial and cultural mixture that prevails in Hawaii is close to that promised land that Dr. King spoke about in his speeches. For the majority of people residing in Hawaii, the diversity of races and cultures is community welcomed and celebrated. This is the environment and atmosphere that became ingrained in the new president, growing up here. My great hope is President Barack Obama can help instill this wonderful community spirit in all of the United States of America.

PART NINE
Women in America

1

The Domination of Women

When I was a preteen, I questioned why my mother and other mothers were deemed inferior to men. I watched how communities, fathers, environments, television, friends, and even how girls treated women and inwardly asked why there was a difference in treatment. Through my experience with American society when I was young, I learned the answer. Women were fighting institutional and social discrimination that existed in American society. Their racial origin did not matter. Our forefathers were all guilty. No one should be a slave to anyone. But slavery still exists in major parts of the world. It should not exist in America, period. As Americans, we should adhere to the fundamental doctrines of change, as allowed by the Constitution and the amendments of legal change. The contributions women make are instrumental to the progress of human life, no matter where they reside, no matter in what country or society that prevails.

When I was a preteen, I perceived a very different treatment of women. But iterating women differently was accepted, just like de facto segregation. At the time, women were viewed as sexual objects and not as humans in a society rift with racial and gender prejudice. Even the law was different. For many years, a woman could not purchase a home without her husband's signature. I saw women beat by their husbands and police who displayed no authority to intervene unless murder occurred. This treatment of women did not just occur in African American communities or ghettos; it was commonplace in all of American society. But change was imminent. Change had to come. And just like African American women in earlier American society, Caucasian women also fought for change. Just like the African Americans, all women strived and demonstrated a strong desire for change.

American society has made major changes concerning how men view women. The glass ceiling has been broken many times, and women are now reaching out to prove that a woman can be the president of the United States of America.

2

Breaking the Discrimination Ceiling

There have been hundreds of women out there who have achieved remarkable and historic precedents. Yes, women have come a long way, but here are some things to consider: at the founding of our country, we know why slaves were not allowed to vote, but why not Caucasian women? Why has our country never had before this century a female president or an African American president of the United States? And why was Hillary Clinton's campaign considered so unusual? Why is our Congress comprised of mostly men? As a society, we need to change our thinking about having a woman president just like we did about having an African American president.

During the journey of Annie's child, I have seen many tremendous and positive changes—especially in 2008 with the Hillary Clinton and the Barack Obama presidential campaigns. The American people, of all races, are voting for change. What a difference now from when I began my journey! I celebrate that Barack Obama has won the nomination and office of president of the United States. However, I also celebrate that a woman and an African American man were the front-runners in our political mandates. When I grew up, such a possibility was deemed impossible. Hillary Clinton came closer to breaking the White House barrier than any woman in history. In the future, it will be unremarkable for a woman to win primary state victories, unremarkable to have a woman in a close race to be a presidential nominee, unremarkable to think that a woman can be president of the United States. And that is truly remarkable. And I envision that it will be unremarkable as well that an African American woman or man can run for and attain the office of president of the United States.

PART TEN
End of Journey?

1

Reverse Discrimination

In Hawaii, we can look at racism from the Caucasian perspective. To paraphrase journalist Tom Brokaw: it has done us little good to communication wire the world if we continue to short-circuit our souls. There is no delete button for racism.

My decision to reside in Hawaii has proved to be a good one. However, the racial disharmony that does display itself at times is disturbing. Hawaii is the only previously monarchal state in the United States. History tells us that Hawaii's most disastrous problems began when the émigré white foreigners or haoles were welcomed to the kingdom. Thus, the embracing of the Americans and the British was the beginning of the end of Hawaii self-rule. Racism and bigotry was influential in the monarchy's demise. Fast-forwarding to the present, racism's shadow still pervades the state of Hawaii. The following article, printed in the local newspaper the *Star-Bulletin*, is a demonstration of racism, sometimes reverse but still present in the state.

By Ken Kobayashi
Star Bulletin

Hawaii Chief Justice Ronald Moon wants lawyers to consider recruiting people of diverse backgrounds to help deal with incidents of discrimination and bigotry that still plague Hawaii. Moon told the Hawaii State Bar Association's young lawyers division yesterday that when he returned to Hawaii after graduating from University of Iowa law school in 1965 to look for a job, Caucasians still controlled hiring practices as a result of the "Big Five" companies that had dominated Hawaii.

He said Asian-American lawyers were not being hired by the white law firms that had controlled most of the legal business here.

Within a few years those law firms hired a "sprinkling" of Asian-Americans, and since then the situation has improved considerably here, Moon said.

Still "an ugly part of this country's legacy is discrimination and bigotry, and Hawaii has not escaped racially or ethnically charged events" He said.

Moon noted that whites comprise 24.3 percent of the population here, which makes them a minority and, some believe, targets of "reverse discrimination."

He cited last year's beating of a Caucasian couple at the Waikele Shopping Center parking lot. A teenager yelled "f---- haole" during the incident, Moon said. He also cited other examples of why lawyers need to fight bigotry:

>> A federal agency found in 2004 that Hilo high school administration failed to address its coaches use of abusive, racially charged language, mishandling of students and threatening a parent.
>> A Honolulu City Councilman, Rod Tam, warned developers that "we don't want wetbacks" working on our city rail projects.
>> The Chief Executive Officer of the Hawaii Tourism Authority, Rex Johnson, resigned after it was learned he used his State computer to e-mail "racist" jokes.

End of article quotation.

Hawaii indeed has its share of racial bigotry, however, the impact for Annie's child is the fact that the verbal racial bigotry heard here does not reflect Hawaii's society the same as in mainland America. Here in Hawaii, bigotry cannot survive, whether institutionally tried or openly espoused. One outstanding reason racism cannot survive in Hawaii is the nonpolarization of the islands. There is no community for racism to survive. Most people living in Hawaii share the "aloha" of cultural and racial diversity. In the Hawaiian isles, the intermingling of the races is a foregone conclusion. Racism cannot proliferate here.

PART ELEVEN
The Newly Elected President of the United States of America

1

The Making of Monumental History

On November 4, 2008, American voters elected a biracial man of African lineage and American Caucasian descent to be the forty-fourth president of the United States! He was also born and partially raised in the state of Hawaii. The election of Barack Obama to president of the United States is a great achievement!

Barack Obama's election to president of the United States assuages institutional racism. I know that Mother Annie is beaming with joy on this historic occasion! At the moment I heard the election results, I immediately remembered the words of Dr. Martin Luther King: "We shall overcome." How ironic, we now have an African American family moving into the White House that was built by the labor of slaves.

This historic occasion does ease the pain for those of us who have had our eyes on the prize—through all the pain and suffering, the marching, the demonstrations, the fire hoses, the dogs, the humiliation, the Ku Klux Klan, and the deaths in the fight for civil rights over the years. The memory and pain of racism will be forever etched in our hearts.

Watching the celebrations on this historic occasion, my tears flowed. Many tears flowed that day, especially from the older generation, and I believe it was an expression of the emotional carriage of suffering from the racism that has been prevalent in America. I know that racism and all of its ugliness will not go away because of this historic occasion.

PART TWELVE
The Local People

1

The History of Racism in Hawaii

When I arrived in Hawaii in 1960, I could sense that Hawaiian residents had a tremendous sympathy for me as an African American because they were aware of our social status on the mainland but not of our progress. But that sympathy provided me with a sense of comfort.

I was, however, surprised at the first racist reference I heard there, which was "that f**king haole." The word *haole* is as much a descriptive as *black* or *white*. Racial descriptions are commonly used in Hawaii. But when you combine the ethnicity with a derogatory word, it becomes a racist term, according to local culture.

Local Hawaiians—and by that I mean to include all the races and cultures residing in the state—intertwine and mix languages, and when the language includes English, it's called pidgin. When I grew up in Chester, Pennsylvania, to describe someone by his or her race was demeaning. So in Hawaii, the word *colored* is not considered derogatory, though it is still tremendously painful to hear, mainly because I remember the Southern signs and common description of African American people. But I make myself understand that as a spoken description in Hawaii it is not meant to be derogatory.

What bothers me also is the casualness with which local people regard these racial epithets toward Caucasian people. Just because it's reverse does not make it right. People sometimes do not realize that the poisonous rhetoric they let their children hear becomes an authoritative okay for the children to act or say derogatory things against others. I have heard that even high school kids in the past have had what they called "kill a haole" day at school. They would deliberately pick a Caucasian person to physically beat for being haole. This action is done, especially with males, to improve their standing with other classmates.

A lot of the scorn shown or spoken by Hawaiian people has been passed down by several generations. There was a time in Hawaiian history where many different races and cultures were treated like slaves. Many of these Native Hawaiians and immigrant people felt the oppression of the Caucasians—most notably, the pineapple and sugarcane field owners. The plantation-type servitude was akin to the slave labor utilized by cotton field owners in the American South. Plantation owners put a lot of injustices and unreasonable demands on the people. The pay was meager, the working hours were long, and the housing was poor. There was little health care or education for the laborers' children.

The biggest insult was the takeover of Hawaii by U.S. government and by local Caucasian businessmen in the 1890s. The queen of Hawaii was forced to abdicate her throne and be imprisoned for a time. Civil rights for local and immigrant Hawaiians was almost extinct. One of the biggest examples of the injustice occurred in the 1930s. There was an openly racist rape case involving a young Caucasian woman, a twenty-year-old wife of a Navy officer. The case kept the attention of the American newspapers for many months. According to the young wife, she was raped by a group of local boys as she was walking though an undeveloped area near Waikiki. The case become more sensational when on January 8, 1932, the young woman's mother, husband, and two other accomplices kidnapped one of the five charged suspects and murdered him. The other four alleged rapists were freed for lack of evidence.

In a spectacular court case that followed, the killers were convicted of manslaughter and later sentenced to ten years of hard labor. But the territorial governor, a haole, commuted their sentences from ten years to one hour—which the prisoners served in his office. This controversial case seriously divided Hawaii's citizens along racial lines for many years. Its judicial outcome still inspires bitter arguments among local people who felt that the "white man's law" had discriminated against darker and poorer local people.

A revelation for me is, this so-called "reverse discrimination" produces the same emotional reaction in me as when I witness whites practicing racism against African American people.

2

Hawaiian Inequality

In the following article, a University of Hawaii professor writes convincingly in the Honolulu weekly newspaper that inequality on the Hawaiian Islands is more prevalent than we like to admit. The article states the question: "Can't We All Just Get Along?"

Hawaii residents often point to the state's racial diversity as a point of pride, and rightly so. According to the U.S. census bureau, minorities make up more than three-fourths of the population. We like to laud the diversity of our islands as something that makes us unique and boast about how well we get along. University of Hawaii's ethic studies professor Jonathan Okamura takes a closer look at the multiculturalism on the islands in "ethnicity and inequality in Hawaii, a 238-page work published by temple university press. He finds that, upon further examination, the model of ethnic relations doesn't appear as sunny as some of its boosters may tout it to be. In "ethnicity and equality" Okamura questions what he calls the "multicultural model" and contends that serious educational, social and economic inequality exists in the State, tied largely to stereotype-rich perceptions of certain ethnic groups like Filipinos and Samoans. Okamura sets out to dispel what he believes is a "simplistic and highly inaccurate" viewpoint that "island society represents a setting of especially tolerant, harmonious and egalitarian ethnic relations and thus can serve as a model for other racially and ethnically diverse societies in managing relations among their constituent groups."

In the end, Okamura convinces this reviewer that the "multicultural model" of ethnic relations in Hawaii has also served as an anesthetizing propaganda model that cloaks the true nature of racism and discrimination on the islands, and that based on the reality of ethnic inequality, this model needs to go.

End of article quotation.

3

Hawaiian Perceptions

Anne's child has gained profound contentment within the diverse racial conglomeration of Hawaii. The emotional scarring suffered during my years as an African American citizen of the United States has healed tremendously since residing in the Hawaii. What can be extracted from the preceding writing depends upon a macro view. The multicultural model does not tell the whole story. Yes, Hawaii is not a perfect racial conglomeration. However, from my life and travel experience, Hawaii comes very close to the "Hollis Johnson" model. The majority of the characteristics of day-to-day intermingling of ethnicities here in Hawaii is mostly positive. And now we have a biracial man—African American and Caucasian mixture—and president of the United States who hails from the state of Hawaii. There are characteristics about the man that exudes a shining example of Hawaiian cultural, racial, and ethnic intermingling.

The following article from the *Washington Post*, published in the *Honolulu Advertiser*, may provide a better view of my feelings about Hawaii and my island neighbors. The article chronicles the twelve-day vacation of the president and his family in Hawaii during the holidays.

4

Understanding the Hawaiian Attitude

Island Influence Seen in Obama's Cool

In his two weeks in Hawaii, Barack Obama oozed island cool: The black shades and khaki shorts, the breezy sandaled saunter that suggested he had not a care in the world.

He strolled shirtless near the beach, enjoyed shave ice and the local seaweed wrapped snack called spam musubi. One day, the resident-elect flashed the friendly shaka sign, shaking his pinky and thumb in a local surfing gesture.

But for the blackberry clipped to his left hip, Obama appeared to be channeling the aloha spirit of his native Hawaii.

Friends here say the country's first island-born-president-elect has long carried more than a touch of the Aloha spirit in his temperament. During the campaign, many admirers suggested that president Obama was too passive in his battles against Hillary Rodham Clinton and John Mccain.

"That's Hawaii", declared representative Neil Abercrombie (D-Hawaii), a contemporary of president Obama's parents who has known the president since-birth.

"You take negative energy and you process it through you and it comes out as positive energy....every time president Obama comes on television now, the collective blood pressure in the United States goes down 10 points. He cools the water. He's sober and he speaks sensibly in a calm manner that breeds confidence".

As president Obama's wife, Michelle, has said, you can't really understand Barack until you understand Hawaii.

Hawaii is no utopia, of course, despite its stunning natural beauty. Tourism drives the state's economy, but many of the jobs it provides are low-wage and low-skill.

"Many people have two or three jobs to make ends meet because it's a very expensive cost of living", said Geoffrey White, chairman of the University of Hawaii's anthropology department. That high cost of living has resulted in a growing homeless population.

There is a theory of behavioral science that people living in the islands behave differently than mainlanders, that on an island competition is not rewarded as well as it is elsewhere. When you live on a rock, on an island, you learn to understand that everyone is critical to the success and survival of that space.

End of article quotation.

PART THIRTEEN
Local People Realities

1

Homelessness

There are areas of Hawaii that are not so beautiful, even with its racial utopia. To see homeless people lying around, pandering, and littering creates a very distasteful view, especially to tourist. If a person is homeless in Hawaii, that person is very fortunate, especially in the environmental sense. I have heard that Hawaii is so popular a place to be homeless that people in that situation have succeeded in getting enough money for a one-way airline ticket to Hawaii to live homelessly. The kindness and generosity of local people has made Hawaii a paradise for the homeless. The homeless are not always people who are irresponsible; on drugs; or have criminal records, shady backgrounds, mental problems, or other personal fallibilities, as studies have shown. I will never forget meeting a gentleman who was a sales clerk at a local utilities and craft store. I was familiar with him as a salesperson for a couple years of going to the store for supplies for my place of employment. We knew each other on a first-name basis, which is not unusual for strangers in the state of Hawaii. As a maintenance engineer in commercial buildings, I relied on his expertise with tools and such to get the correctly needed merchandise for major maintenance or repair work.

Then one day I went to the store and got the shocking news that he had died. One of his co-workers explained to me the circumstance of his death. I learned that he had been homeless during the whole time that I had known him and had been murdered during an apparent robbery as he slept in his makeshift shelter! I learned that he had lost his home some time ago as a result of a divorce. I was told that he could not afford the increase in the lease on an apartment and became homeless.

Annie's child can mentally and emotionally weld with the homeless. Back in February 1960, I spent a brief period living with the homeless on the streets of downtown Los Angeles. I was at the time attending military construction school at the Seabee base in Port Hueneme, California. A future wife, Patricia, the mother of my two children, Andrea and Donald, was attending college in Los Angeles. By coincidence, she had moved to Los Angeles to live with her aunt and to advance her education at the same time that I was transferred to California for military Seabee construction training. We did not marry until May of that year, so we were still dating.

The base where I was stationed was sixty miles north of Los Angeles. I would visit with Patricia on the weekends, usually arriving Friday evenings by a bus from Port Hueneme and a cable car from downtown Los Angeles. I would usually stay at a downtown hotel after visiting Patricia and her aunt for the evening. Those were really nice weekends for the two of us. We would take trips to various places on the weekends, including the recently opened Disneyland.

It was very interesting talking with various people on the trip back from my girlfriend's house to downtown by cable car. I became deeply aware of the homeless people I would pass on the street in that downtown Los Angeles area. I would contribute small amounts of money to those who solicited me. I felt sorry for their situation and for the fact that they were African American. There was one exception though. I noticed on several occasions that one of the homeless guys would ask me for money for the white lady. I finally figured it out one day when I saw an elderly Caucasian lady pushing her cart in the area. As I passed by the group, I heard her chastising two of them. The two guys had eaten some of her watermelon she had on the cart.

Another day when I walked by the area, I noticed that the group was pointing at me. I waved as usual to say hello and to my surprise they all waved back. As fate would have it, I would soon be living with them! The next week, the school I was attending had a week of closure. So I took military leave until the following Friday, when I had to report back to the base command. It was getting pretty close to payday, and I was feeling the stress of not having too much money. I bought my round-trip bus ticket, made the reservation for the weekend at the hotel, and went to Los Angeles. Because of my lack of money, Patricia and I stuck close to her home, sightseeing in the area. She had requested that I bring my Navy uniform with me so we could get pictures together.

I usually left my return portion of my round-trip bus ticket in my hotel room, but this time I had forgotten to do that. I remember seeing the bus ticket in my wallet during our sightseeing trip to the tar pit area. But I learned on Saturday night after returning to my hotel room that I had somehow lost the ticket. Imagine my dismay when I did not have enough money left to pay for a bus ticket back to Port Hueneme. I had to get some money for a bus ticket by Monday morning.

I was young and too embarrassed to ask for money from my girlfriend or her aunt. I went to the bus station, hoping they would give me a credit pass, but I was told they could not do that without their manager's approval, and he was out of town until the following Friday. I had to check out of the hotel by Monday morning. That Sunday night, sitting in the room, I had the idea of hitchhiking back to the base. It would be a lot easier to hitch a ride in uniform. In those days, people respected and loved to help guys in uniform. That was not true a few years later during the anti–Vietnam War protest. It was actually considered dangerous, and some military commanders even recommended uniforms not be worn off base. I had to figure out a hitchhiking strategy to get to the main highway going back to Port Hueneme.

When I checked out of the hotel that Monday morning, I knew I had a long road ahead. As I walked along the street down from the hotel, I passed the area where the homeless usually could be seen. There were five men there that I was familiar with seeing. These guys were fifty years old or older. One of them recognized me and hollered, "Hey, sailor!" I replied but kept walking. Then the guy asked me, "Are you really in the Navy?" I responded that I was, and the five of them gathered around me.

Their response made me feel proud and important. I felt like a movie star. As my conversation with these men continued, I felt honored by them. Some of the stories I heard from them was astounding—especially one from a World War II veteran. He enlightened me about how "colored" servicemen inside the United States were treated at that time. He stated that when he was serving in France and Italy, the French and Italians treated African American servicemen as people, and he had never experienced the "separation of the races" rules in those countries as was common in America.

As I continued my conversation with these men, I started to feel like one of the group. Each person explained their different experiences that led them to that moment in their lives. I began to appreciate how far my parents had gotten with a sixth-grade education—all that was allowed for African Americans living in the state of Mississippi. When I told these guys about my plans to hitchhike back to my base, they suggested that I go get breakfast with them. I was shocked when they asked me about breakfast, because I could only imagine what breakfast would be for homeless people. When I said yes, the guys were elated, and I wondered if I had gotten myself into a real mess.

They all had nicknames, and I can still remember "Limpy"— called that because he limped because of a World War II injury. Limpy stated that we would all go to church after we found the white woman. I remembered her and asked about her status among them. The guys spoke highly of her. She was near sixty years old and was originally from Alabama. When I heard the word *Alabama,* I thought inwardly, "This is not possible, a white woman from Alabama being friends with these Negro men." I had witnessed in my short lifetime "Negro" men and boys being murdered for only speaking to or smiling at a white woman in the South.

As we walked through the alleyways to find her, the guys told me the story of how she ended up homeless on the streets of Los Angeles. Her son and husband had both died during World War II. Her husband's life, they said, was once saved by three "Negro" men in the battlefields of Italy. Her son was in the U.S. Navy and was killed on a ship that was sunk by Japanese warplanes near Okinawa. The white lady ended up moving to Los Angeles to live with her sister, who was her only remaining family. She and her sister became estranged later, from what I could understand, because of her positive feelings about "colored" people. I never did get the full details about that part of her life.

I was beginning to feel like family with these guys. When we came upon the white lady—Emily, as I found out her name later—was asleep in her cart in the alleyway. I have to say the smell of homelessness—the smell of decomposing garbage—was very pronounced in that alleyway, but I was getting used to it. One of the guys awakened her, and she asked, "You are a sailor?"

I explained to her that I was not a shipboard sailor and that I was training to be in Navy construction. I explained that I was trying to get back to my Navy base. Emily was full of questions, and I enjoyed talking to her. One of the guys explained to her that I was hungry for some breakfast. I wondered why they had to rely on her about breakfast. I found out, as we were walking to the church, that she was the only person who could get "colored" people into the church for eating. As we came upon this large church, the guys explained to me that Emily was the only one who could get them into the church because usually the church feeds only the white homeless. I found out later, from the clergyman, that Emily had been furious when she found out about this "whites only" policy and had spoken directly to the clergyman operating the feeding program. He assured her that, if she could get Negro people to attend the sermons before meals are served, it would be no problem.

This church was dedicated to feeding and converting the homeless to Christianity. We had to listen to the church program and the sermon of the pastor before we got to eat. In what I know now was a very good idea, after breakfast we also had to help the volunteers in the kitchen clean up and prepare for the next meal.

Emily was smitten by me. She kept talking to me, sticking close to me, and relating to me her late son's Navy experiences. As Emily and I talked on the way back to her living area, Emily was shocked that I had no bus ticket to get back to my Navy base. She told me that she would fix the problem and get me back to the base by Friday. I felt confident that she would find a way. So I resigned myself to living with the homeless for a few days.

It was a moving experience. The experience of sleeping together in alleyways, the begging techniques, and most surprisingly the desire the homeless demonstrated in being helpful to each other. Emily was the one who suggested that I not beg for money. She was really determined to help me herself. Living two nights and two days on the streets felt like a lifetime. That Wednesday morning, I felt like I could not take that kind of living anymore. I felt stinky and dirty. Fortunately, the church kept outhouses near the church for homeless use. Emily came to me that morning and asked me to bring my duffel bag and go with her for a walk. I asked if I could push her cart for her, and she said, "No way. You're a Navy man, not a bum like me."

I said to her, "Please don't say that. You're not a bum but a human being."

Emily squeezed my hand tightly, looked up into my eyes, and said, "You are my son."

I felt honored to hear her say those words. As Emily and I turned the corner, I realized that we were heading toward the bus station. It was at that point I realized she must have gotten me the bus fare money, and I asked, "You got the bus fare money, didn't you?"

She said, "No, I got you a ticket back to Port Hueneme."

I wondered how she came up with the forty-six dollars to pay for the ticket. I felt terribly relieved and appreciative.

She hurried me on. "Go, go."

I hugged her, kissed her face, and said, "Thank you so much."

And she said, "Go, my son."

Before walking away, I said, "I'll pay you back, and I'll come visit with you each time I come to Los Angeles." As I was walking away, I thought about my own mother, Annie, and began remembering when I turned around to take a last glimpse of Mother Annie standing at the door, watching me walk away. Before entering the bus station door, I turned to look back at Emily. She waved at me, and I could tell she was crying, as she wiped her face with an old cloth. As I rode the bus back to Port Hueneme, I felt so helpless that I could not help her and the other homeless.

I did go back to see her and the other guys on each visit to Los Angeles and spent some time with them. I tried to give the money back to Emily, but she refused to accept a payback. I instead used the money to buy them all canned foods, which started a habit for me. Each time I visited, I brought cans of food in my military duffel bag. They always referred to me as the sailor man, but Emily always called me her son. Unfortunately, I never had the chance to spend much time with her as a son.

As time passed, I graduated from military school and received military orders to transfer to U.S. Naval Station Midway Island. Patricia and I decided to get married before I left to go to the base. We received permission from our parents, and her aunt set up a marriage ceremony for us at her house in west Los Angeles. A minister married us, and we honeymooned in downtown Los Angeles while staying at the Ambassador Hotel. I was due for transfer to Midway Island in a week's time. While staying at the hotel, Patricia and I visited our homeless friends each time we left or came back from a trip that week. Patricia and I went to the church sermons and worked in the kitchen with them that week. Emily was so pleased by our visits. She even managed to get small wedding gifts for both of us. I still have this many years later, the small pinky ring she gave me as a gift. Saying good-bye to that small group of homeless people brought me to tears.

While I was on Midway Island, Patricia and I, through correspondence, decided she would transfer back to a school in Pennsylvania. She would leave with me after I returned to Los Angeles on leave. She decided to live with her parents while I served my time in the military.

When I returned to Los Angeles, after completing my tour of duty on Midway Island, I took a trip downtown with my wife to visit "Mom" and the others. Just viewing the nestling area of my homeless friends, I realized something wasn't the same. There were tents set up, and the area was a lot cleaner. The faces there were not familiar, and we continued to walk down the alleyway until finally I came upon two familiar faces, Limpy and Joe. It felt great seeing them again, and they remembered us right away. But there was good and bad news from them. Three of their group had ended up in jail for buying and selling drugs in a police sting operation. And according to Limpy, the white lady went back to Alabama. Her sister died and left Emily her Los Angeles home in a will. Emily sold the home and moved back to Alabama to live with a distant relative. I never got a hold of her, even though I tried later. I did not have enough information about her to locate her. Limpy told me that after I left for Midway Island she would say often that she would see her sailor son again and that she would live in a decent home someday. That provided me with some consolation. My experience from living with the homeless for a couple of days helped me cope mentally with the disadvantages of being involved in the Vietnam War.

When I finally retired from the military and came to Hawaii to begin a new career, I could not forget my homeless experience and learning that the homeless are people too—many of whom have suffered from misfortune. After I began a chief building engineering career in Hawaii, I became an advocate for food drives within the commercial buildings where I worked to help the Hawaii Food Bank. Each time we spearheaded these food drives, I would think of "Mother" Emily.

There are many rescue areas for the homeless in Hawaii. There is the fabulous Hawaii Food Bank shelter programs, feeding kitchens, and volunteers who deliver food to the Hawaii State's overall homeless culture; the aloha spirit exists in trying to resolve the problems of the homeless. Even many tourists have taken time out to help the homeless during their vacation time.

Homelessness can create unsightly messes, especially in our parks and on our beaches. Local Hawaiian people realize that seeing the homeless in Hawaii is not good, but do appreciate that it could be worse. Hawaii's authorities are doing their best to remedy the homeless problem. From the state government, city councils, and ordinary volunteers, the best is being done. Lee Cataluna, a columnist with the *Honolulu Advertiser* newspaper, wrote about compassion not being a simple thing in the real world. She explains that most of the homeless are not afraid of breaking the law or going to jail. Prison means having hot meals, clean bedding, and shelter. She explains that there are many factors contributing to the continued increase of the homeless in the state of Hawaii. It will be our job as Hawaiian citizens to find a solution that works for all of us—the homeless is fine example.

2

Expectoration

When you work in certain public areas of Hawaii, you observe the behavior of people in many forms. One ugly observation is people spitting. Yes, I mean spitting from the mouth. In many public areas of Hawaii, men, women, and children can be observed spitting on the sidewalks and roadways. It is an ugliness that seems very well accepted by local people—unless, of course, you are like me and grew up in a society that did not deem spitting in public as an acceptable behavior. These local people who spit are observed by their children, and the children get the impression that this action is proper. Soon the children will resort to the same behavior. Expectoration exists within the overall culture of Hawaii people.

Perhaps one of the reasons it bothers me so much carries back to my childhood. When I read the essay in high school that offended the teacher and some of the students, I had a white classmate, Jane, who praised me for reading it. As she walked out of the classroom, I watched as two other female classmates spit in her face and called her a "nigger lover." I have felt deeply offended about spitting ever since.

3

Expletives Not Deleted

Another irritant to my being is hearing the expletive f**k. The word is used in conversations by most local people in Hawaii. This expletive is sometimes used as part of normal conversation. From my observation, this particular expletive is spoken as if it were some kind of rite of passage among the younger generation. The people who express this expletive—by their mannerisms and body language—seem to think that using this word makes their statements more convincing or more important. I deplore hearing expletives, which I heard quite often during my military career. As a child, using expletives was something you didn't dare use in the presence of adults. I know that this expletive is common in America, not just Hawaii. When I grew up, this particular expletive was used only as a description for sex acts and not as common language as it is used today. What is deplorable is to hear young people, especially teenagers, using this word.

What sickens me the most is to hear mothers and fathers use the expletive to curse at their children. They don't seem to realize that each time the child hears these curse expletives they are reinforcing the use of this expletive. Cursing becomes a normal function to a child. Expletives are even common in movies now. I realize that expletives cannot be eradicated in a nation that has free speech as birthright, but forming the character of a child need not involve instilling expletives.

PART FOURTEEN
Statehood

1

The Commemoration

Although racism, prejudice, and discrimination have wreaked havoc on the soul of Annie's child through the years, I now reside in a state where the environment allowed for an emotional healing process. I reside in a state that helped produce the first president of the United States born with African heritage.

Although the overt racism, prejudice, and discrimination does not exist in today's Hawaii, there was a time when that same foul racism wrecked havoc on the Native Hawaiian people and culture, just the same as the American Indian. The year 2009 marks the fiftieth year since Hawaii became an American state. There is much to lament and much to celebrate. I think that the monumental occasion was best described in an article published by Mark Niesse, Associated Press, as follows:

Capitol Commemorates 1959 Admission Act.

Legislators, notables, protesters mark 50 years since signing.

The state that gave America it's first black president was hailed as a model of tolerance and diversity on the 50th anniversary of president Dwight Eisenhower's signing of the bill that eventually led to Hawaii becoming the 50th state.

The pen Eisenhower used was on display at the State Capitol as past and present state leaders sang Hawaiian music in the State house chamber, held hands and reflected in speeches yesterday on the meaning of joining the United States.

The Hawaii admission act was signed March 18th 1959, clearing the way for a vote by Hawaii residents in June and the islands acceptance into the nation August 21.

Statehood was the result of a long series of events: the 1893 overthrow of the Hawaiian monarchy, the island's years as a remote U.S. territory and their importance in the pacific following the attack on Pearl Harbor during World War II.

Speeches commemorating the 50th anniversary emphasized the Island's ethnic diversity and their right to have a voice in the United States through the overwhelming 93 percent vote for statehood.

"Statehood is a fraud', said one longtime protester, who carried his Hawaii flag upside down as a sign of distress.

Others with the Hawaiian independence action alliance said they feared that the island's native people will lose what's left of their sovereignty if the U.S. congress passes a pending measure that would give them a degree of self government similar to that of the American Indians.

But the State congressional house speaker, told the audience in his speech that Hawaii embraces core American ideals of overcoming adversity and accepting different cultures, as shown by the State's election of the nation's first Chinese, Japanese and Hawaiian Senators and it being the birthplace of President Barack Obama.

End of article quotation.

Part Fifteen
Annie's Child: Hawaii

1

An American Remedy

Annie's child wishes the best to all who are going through the healing process, the process of restoring stolen self-confidence and self-esteem from within your emotions. Racial injustice took its toll on me. America's past racial injustice to African Americans has been significantly abolished. Try to move on. Racial justice is becoming a part of American living, thanks largely to the advent of the U.S. Constitution and U.S. citizens who took a stand against violations of human rights. All of America can use the state of Hawaii and its multiethnic, multicultural population as an example for racial harmony. Hawaii is an outstanding model for human interaction within the confines of the United States.

2

The Healing

For Annie's child, the healing process for the emotional scarring caused by the racism has progressed. True healing began after I moved to Hawaii. I only began to realize the affects of racism upon me after my assimilation into Hawaii's culture. Thank you, Hawaiian culture, for aloha!

3

Family Reunion 2009

I recently took a visit to Mother Annie's home in Dover, Delaware, to celebrate Mother's Day 2009 with her. It was a wonderful visit! It turned into a family reunion with her and all of my living siblings. During the time I spent visiting my mother and other family, one of my brothers escorted me around the old Chester Township neighborhood where we once lived. We spent a lot of hours there, seeing neighboring families we once knew and sightseeing in the area. While visiting Chester again, I did not feel the emotional frustration about the racial stigma I had suffered growing up there. People of many different races intermingle in that area now. The whole county seems so different now in regard to racial acceptance. Race relations seem so improved by the way people of different races have positive interaction with each other.

Epilogue

Mother Annie, Annie Clara Mcnair Johnson, resides in Dover, Delaware.

Annie's child, Hollis Earl Johnson, resides in Mililani, Honolulu, Hawaii.

My siblings (except Tommie Jean, deceased since 1992) have all enjoyed numerous family reunions in recent years. Cousins, nieces, nephews, aunts, uncles, and other relatives have joined the occasions.

One of my most enjoyable ventures in Hawaii occurred when I learned that my nephew—my late sister Jean's only child, Michael—had arrived and was residing in Honolulu County, Hawaii. When I last saw him, he had only been four months old. I had seen pictures of him but never met him until he moved to Hawaii. Living only a few miles from me, our relationship has blossomed, and I see so much of my best friend Jean in his demeanor. Michael was Mother Annie's first grandchild. He was raised in my mother and father's household after I departed on life's adventure.

It has been a long road to the relief felt by Annie's child. Mother Annie instilled in me an ounce of fortitude that became a major muscle for withstanding the emotional pain of racism. The ravages of racism that almost destroyed the self-esteem, self-worth, and emotional stability of Annie's child are subtle now.

I now live in a different, outstandingly positive world of racial interaction. Dr. Martin Luther King Jr., your dream is still alive, and America is getting there!

To my siblings, Tommie Jean, Brook Fontane, Leslie Andrew, Teresa Ann, Anita Louise, Timothy Leon, Doren Michele,

To my children, Donald Jay and Andrea Denene,

Thank you for your understanding, love and support!

Family Descendants

1. Grandfather: Les Mcnair (deceased 1979).
2. Grandmother: Estella Polk Mcnair (deceased 1974).
3. Mother: Annie Clara Mcnair Johnson (born April 1925). Now residing in Dover, Delaware.
4. Father: Tommie Lee Johnson (born November 1920; deceased December 1997).
5. First Born. Son: Hollis Earl Johnson (born August 1941). Now residing in Hawaii.
6. Second Born. Daughter: Tommie Jean Johnson (born January 1943; deceased 1992).
7. Third Born. Son: Brook Fontane Johnson (born August 1945). Now residing in Boothwyn, Pennsylvania.
8. Fourth Born. Son: Leslie Andrew Johnson (born April 1948). Now residing in Sharon Hill, Pennsylvania.
9. Fifth Born. Daughter: Teresa Ann Johnson (born October 1950). Now residing in Sharon Hill, Pennsylvania.
10. Sixth Born. Daughter: Anita Louise Johnson (born April 1952). Now residing in New Castle, Delaware.
11. Seventh Born. Son: Timothy Leon Johnson (born September 1953). Now residing in Newtown Square, Pennsylvania.
12. Eighth Born. Daughter: Doren Michele Johnson (born October 10, 1955). Now residing in Dover, Delaware.

Description Clockwise.

1. Mother Annie at age 26.
2. Mother Annie at age 22.
3. Mother Annie and son Hollis going to the dance floor on July 15, 2000.
4. Two of Mother Annie's sisters, Loretta (left) and Eudora (right), as preteens. Picture taken in 1942.
5. Mother Annie and son Hollis going to dance floor at family reunion.

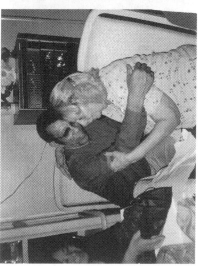

1. Annie's father, Les Mcnair, and mother, Estella Mcnair. Picture taken in the 1960s in Mount Olive, Mississippi. Les Mcnair has a dark tan; however, he is of pure Irish descent. Estella Mcnair is of Choctaw Indian and Nigerian descent.
2. The three surviving sisters (as of 2009). At left, Estella; center is Mother Annie; and at right is Eudora.
3. Mother Annie, picture taken in 1988 in Mount Olive, Mississippi.
4. Mother Annie and son Hollis at family reunion in the year 2000.

1. Mother Annie's daughter Tommie Jean (now deceased) at her wedding in 1960.
2. The Mcnair Family together in 1959. This family reunion was prompted by the death of one brother. Mother Annie is in the center of the picture. Aunt Loretta is seated to the left of her mother, Estella, and sister Eudora is on the end of the picture.
3. Mother Annie and son Hollis during the family reunion in the year 2000.

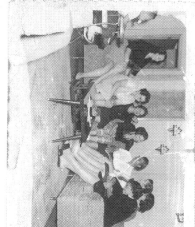

1. Mother Annie in Jackson, Mississippi, in 1989.
2. All of the Mcnair daughters and Mother Estella seated together at a family reunion in 1959.
3. Mother Annie in Jackson, Mississippi, in 1989.